THIS BOOK IS DEDICATED TO DR. MICHAEL HEGGERTY, WHOSE VISION AND EXPERTISE INSPIRES US EVERYDAY.

**Why We Wrote This Book:**

As reading specialists, we worked with struggling readers to provide intervention support, and we had the privilege of working with Michael Heggerty as our mentor. Dr. Heggerty created the PreK, Kindergarten and Primary curricula to be used in Tier 1 instruction, however, we know that older students who struggle with word reading will benefit from explicit instruction in phonemic awareness. While this is not often part of Tier 1 instruction, it is an essential and often missing piece for struggling readers.

The intervention lessons are based on the work of Dr. Michael Heggerty, and his Phonemic Awareness curriculum that has been part of Pre-K, Kindergarten, and Primary classrooms over the last 20 years.

ABOUT THE AUTHORS:

**Alisa VanHekken** is the Chief Academic Officer at Literacy Resources and had the privilege of serving as one of the Reading Specialists who worked with Michael Heggerty and worked alongside him as the Reading Specialist Coordinator. She has also taught Kindergarten and 1st grade. Alisa lives in the suburbs of Chicago with her husband and their 3 daughters.

**Marjorie Bottari** is currently a literacy specialist for Heggerty Phonemic Awareness. She has served as a classroom teacher, reading specialist, literacy coach, administrator and adjunct professor. She had the honor of working closely with Michael Heggerty when she was a reading specialist. Michael also served as her mentor when she received her administrative degree. Marjorie lives in the suburbs of Chicago with her husband, two children, and her super cute dog.

ISBN 978-1-947260-28-3 | v0221 | For more information please visit our website: www.heggerty.org

# Bridge the Gap: At-A-Glance

Phonemic Awareness is the understanding that spoken words are made up of individual sounds called phonemes. A learner who is phonemically aware understands words are made up of sounds, however, a learner who has phonemic proficiency is able to isolate sounds, blend, segment and manipulate the individual sounds in words.

**PURPOSE OF THIS CURRICULUM:**

This curriculum was written as a resource to be used during an intervention lesson, focusing the instruction specifically on developing phonemic awareness. The phonemic awareness lessons can be part of an intervention lesson that also incorporates instruction in phonics and opportunities for connected (decodable or controlled) text reading.

This curriculum was designed to help teachers provide targeted instruction for students who are not yet proficient with phonemic awareness.

**INTENDED AUDIENCE:**

The lessons are meant to bridge the gap and target instruction for students in 2nd grade and above who struggle to decode or encode words in print. These lessons are designed to be part of a Tier 2 or Tier 3 intervention. Lessons can be taught one-on-one or within a small group (5 learners or less).

**HOW TO USE THIS CURRICULUM:**

This curriculum has three parts that increase in level of difficulty.

> **CURRICULUM STRUCTURE:**
>
> Part 1: Phoneme Isolation: Initial, Final, & Medial Phonemes
>
> Part 2: Blending and Segmenting: Syllables and Phonemes
>
> Part 3: Phoneme Manipulation: Adding, Deleting and Substituting Phonemes in Words

Lessons were designed to target specific needs in phonemic awareness instruction. After administering the Placement Assessment, identify where to begin using the Scoring Guide on page 13.

Phoneme isolation, blending, and segmenting are prerequisite skills for phoneme manipulation. If a student scores below 80% in part 1 and/or 2, instruction should focus on phoneme isolation, blending and/or segmenting prior to phoneme manipulation.

The lessons are meant to be 5-7 minutes of your intervention time.

The Phonemic Awareness lessons are oral and auditory, and the words in each lesson are not shown in print.

# Bridge the Gap: At-A-Glance

The Bridge the Gap lessons include explicit instruction in early, basic, and advanced phonemic awareness skills. Teachers may find that students need instruction in multiple phonemic awareness skills at the same time. However, a student should be proficient in early and basic phonemic awareness skills before moving to advanced skills (phoneme manipulation).

**LESSON FOCUS:** When working with the lessons, a lesson focus is provided, along with teacher administration directions. Teachers may choose to explicitly share the lesson focus with learners for each lesson.

**ANCHOR LESSONS:** Anchor lessons have been provided for each skill, along with a reciprocal teaching structure for instruction. It includes explicit instruction for the phonemic awareness skills and activities that can be used to provide instruction and support for all learners. The anchor lessons include a teacher model (I Do), an opportunity to work together (We Do), and then an opportunity for students to practice the skill on their own (You Do).

**TEACHER TIPS:** Throughout the lessons, you will find Teacher Tips and suggestions for scaffolding support for learners. Teachers can use their professional judgment to determine if more or less support is necessary for an individual learner or a small group of learners.

**HAND MOTIONS:** Hand motions for the skills are listed but they are not required for all learners. If students are able to complete the task without the visual support (hand motion and/or colored squares or tiles), this demonstrates phonemic proficiency. Teachers do not need to require all students to use the hand motions.

**ASSESSMENTS:** Assessments have been included within the curriculum and can be used to monitor student progress and determine if additional instruction is needed for a learner or group of learners, before moving onto the next set of lessons.

The Placement Assessment (included on pages 5-13) can be used to determine where to begin instruction. The same assessment can be re-administered after completion of the intervention lessons to analyze student progress and determine next steps.

Assessments can also be downloaded at www.heggerty.org/btg

**QR CODES:** QR codes found on Anchor Lessons link to hand motion videos.

# Why would phonemic awareness be part of an intervention lesson?

Students who struggle to decode benefit from explicit instruction in phonemic awareness and phonics. The lessons included in this curriculum provide systematic and explicit instruction in the sounds we hear in spoken words.

Most classrooms teach phonemic awareness in Kindergarten and 1st grade as Tier 1 instruction, so older learners may receive instruction in Phonemic Awareness (PA) during an intervention. The PA lessons are an oral warm up and can take place prior to phonics instruction and connected (decodable or controlled) text reading.

---

The following research highlights the importance of phonemic awareness, as part of an intervention lesson that focuses on foundational reading skills for students who struggle to decode words automatically and accurately.

"Before children can use a knowledge of sound-spelling relationships to decode words, they must understand that words are made up of sounds" (Adams, 1990).

"Research on word reading processes has distinguished several ways to read words." (Ehri, 1991, 1994).

"The process of decoding words never read before involves transforming graphemes into phonemes and then blending the phonemes to form words with recognizable meanings. The PA skill centrally involved in decoding is blending." (National Reading Panel report 2000, 2-11)

"In each of these studies with highly effective outcomes, researchers provided intensive phonemic awareness training (to the advanced level), intensive phonic decoding training, and substantial opportunity for reading connected text." (Kilpatrick, 2015)

"Phoneme awareness performance is a strong predictor of long-term reading and spelling success, and it can predict literacy performance more accurately than variables such as intelligence, vocabulary knowledge, and socioeconomic status." (Gillon, 2018)

"It is likely that classroom-level instruction in phonological awareness, by itself, will not be sufficient to prevent reading disabilities in children who have serious deficiencies in phonological processing (Torgesen, in press). These children will require more intensive, detailed, and explicit instruction to achieve the level of phonemic awareness required to support reading growth." (Torgesen & Mathes, 2000)

# Phonemic Awareness Placement Assessment for Bridge the Gap Intervention Lessons

Student Name: _____    Placement Assessment Date: _____

Post Assessment Date: _____

This assessment may be administered to students in 2nd grade and above to determine where to begin instruction using Bridge the Gap: Phonemic Awareness Intervention Lessons.

Directions: Mark correct response with a +. Mark incorrect response with a dash (-) and record the incorrect response. Use the scoring guide at the end to identify where to begin instruction. The same assessment may be used as a post test to monitor student growth and determine next steps.

*If the student is unable to give a correct response within 4 seconds, the administrator can move onto the next assessment word.*

## PART 1: PHONEME ISOLATION

### Phoneme Isolation: Isolate the Initial Sound

Teacher Administration Directions: I will say a word and isolate the first sound in the word. The word is popcorn. The first sound we hear in the word "popcorn" is /p/. Can you repeat this back to me: popcorn, /p/?

Now it's your turn. What is the first sound you hear in the word "rainbow"?

| CORRECT RESPONSE: | Yes, /r/ is the first sound we hear in the word "rainbow". |
|---|---|
| INCORRECT RESPONSE: | /r/, "rainbow". /r/ is the first sound we hear in the word "rainbow". |

Teacher Note: If a student responds with the letter name rather than the letter sound say, "That is a letter name. What is the first sound you hear?"

| | WORD: | CORRECT RESPONSE: | STUDENT RESPONSE: | PLACEMENT SCORE: | STUDENT RESPONSE: | POST SCORE: |
|---|---|---|---|---|---|---|
| 1 | number | /n/ | | | | |
| 2 | astronaut | /ă/ | | | | |
| 3 | luggage | /l/ | | | | |
| 4 | eager | /ē/ | | | | |
| 5 | joyful | /j/ | | | | |
| 6 | awesome | /aw/ | | | | |
| | | | Score: /6 | | | |

## Phoneme Isolation: Isolate the Final Sound

Teacher Administration Directions: I will say a word and isolate the final or last sound in the word. The word is "lime". The last sound we hear in the word "lime" is /m/. Can you repeat this back to me: lime, /m/?

Now it's your turn. What is the last sound you hear in the word "seat"?

| CORRECT RESPONSE: | Yes, /t/ is the last sound we hear in the word "seat". |
|---|---|
| INCORRECT RESPONSE: | Seat, /t/. /t/ is the last sound we hear in "seat". |

Teacher Note: If a student responds with the letter name rather than the letter sound say, "That is a letter name. What is the last sound you hear?"

| | WORD: | CORRECT RESPONSE: | STUDENT RESPONSE: | PLACEMENT SCORE: | STUDENT RESPONSE: | POST SCORE: |
|---|---|---|---|---|---|---|
| 1 | rattle | /l/ | | | | |
| 2 | vanish | /sh/ | | | | |
| 3 | peanuts | /s/ | | | | |
| 4 | wrist | /t/ | | | | |
| 5 | player | /er/ | | | | |
| 6 | overlap | /p/ | | | | |
| | | | Score: /6 | | | |

## Phoneme Isolation: Isolate the Medial Sound

Teacher Administration Directions: I will say a word and I will isolate the middle or vowel sound in that word. The word is "plant." The middle or vowel sound I hear in the word "plant" is /ă/. Can you say that: plant /ă/?

Now it's your turn. I will say a word and you will repeat it: "sleep". What is the middle or vowel sound you hear in the word "sleep"?

| CORRECT RESPONSE: | Yes, /ē/ is the middle/vowel sound you hear in the word "sleep". |
|---|---|
| INCORRECT RESPONSE: | Sleep, /ē/. /ē/ is the middle/vowel sound you hear in the word "sleep." |

| | WORD: | CORRECT RESPONSE: | STUDENT RESPONSE: | PLACEMENT SCORE: | STUDENT RESPONSE: | POST SCORE: |
|---|---|---|---|---|---|---|
| 1 | brisk | /i/ | | | | |
| 2 | choice | /oi/ | | | | |
| 3 | blend | /ĕ/ | | | | |
| 4 | deep | /ē/ | | | | |
| 5 | north | /or/ | | | | |
| 6 | zoom | /oo/ | | | | |
| | | | Score: /6 | | | |

## PART 2: BLENDING & SEGMENTING

### Blending Syllables: (Teacher can use chopping hand motion to show the syllables.)

Teacher Administration Directions:  I will say the syllables in a word and blend the syllables together to say the whole word.  /hab/-/ĭ/-/tat/; when I blend the syllables, /hab/-/ĭ/-/tat/, the word is habitat.

Now it's your turn.  Listen to these syllables and tell me the whole word: /re/-/mem/-/ber/.  What is the word?

| CORRECT RESPONSE: | Yes, when you blend the syllables /re/-/mem/-/ber/, the word is remember. |
|---|---|
| INCORRECT RESPONSE: | Listen, when you blend the syllables, /re/-/mem/-/ber/, the word is remember.  Say it back to me: /re/-/mem/-/ber/, remember. |

| | SYLLABLES: | CORRECT RESPONSE: | STUDENT RESPONSE: | PLACEMENT SCORE: | STUDENT RESPONSE: | POST SCORE: |
|---|---|---|---|---|---|---|
| 1 | cū - cum - ber | cucumber | | | | |
| 2 | pret - zel | pretzel | | | | |
| 3 | im - por - tant | important | | | | |
| 4 | gē - ŏm - mĭ - tree | geometry | | | | |
| 5 | maj - ĭ - cal | magical | | | | |
| 6 | sub - trac - tion | subtraction | | | | |
| | | | Score:    /6 | | | |

### Blending Phonemes: (Teacher can use chopping hand motion to show the syllables.)

Teacher Administration Directions:  I will say the sounds in a word and blend those sounds together to say the whole word. Listen. /k – ī - t/, kite. When I blend those 3 sounds together, /k – ī - t/, the word is kite.

Now it's your turn.  Listen to these sounds and tell me the whole word: /p - ĕ- t/. What is the word?

| CORRECT RESPONSE: | Yes, when you blend the sounds, /p – ĕ - t/, the word is pet. |
|---|---|
| INCORRECT RESPONSE: | Listen, when you blend the 3 sounds, /p – ĕ - t/, the word is pet.  Say it back to me: /p – ĕ - t/, pet. |

| | PHONEMES: | CORRECT RESPONSE: | STUDENT RESPONSE: | PLACEMENT SCORE: | STUDENT RESPONSE: | POST SCORE: |
|---|---|---|---|---|---|---|
| 1 | p - or - ch | porch | | | | |
| 2 | h - oi - s - t | hoist | | | | |
| 3 | m – ĭ – s - t | mist | | | | |
| 4 | s - p – l – ă - sh | splash | | | | |
| 5 | s - l - e - p - t | slept | | | | |
| 6 | g – r – oo – p | group | | | | |
| | | | Score:    /6 | | | |

**Segmenting Words into Syllable:** (Student can use chopping hand motion to show syllables.)

Teacher Administration Directions: I will say a word and I will segment the word into the syllables I hear.

Listen. Survival, /sur/-/vī/-/val/. I hear 3 syllables in survival, /sur/-/vī/ -/val/.

Now it's your turn. The word is "forgiven." What are the syllables you hear in the word "forgiven?"

| | | |
|---|---|---|
| CORRECT RESPONSE: | Yes, when you segment the word forgiven into syllables, you hear /for/-/gĭv/-/en/. |
| INCORRECT RESPONSE: | When I segment the word forgiven into syllables, I hear 3 syllables, /for/-/gĭv/-/en/. Say it back to me: forgiven, /for/-/gĭv/-/en/. |

| | WORD: | CORRECT RESPONSE: | STUDENT RESPONSE: | PLACEMENT SCORE: | STUDENT RESPONSE: | POST SCORE: |
|---|---|---|---|---|---|---|
| 1 | trampoline | tram - pō - line | | | | |
| 2 | intelligence | in - tel - ĭ - gence | | | | |
| 3 | conversation | con - ver - sā - tion | | | | |
| 4 | introduce | in - trō - duce | | | | |
| 5 | salamander | sal - ŭ - man - der | | | | |
| 6 | registration | reg - ĭ - strā - tion | | | | |
| | | | Score: /6 | | | |

**Segmenting Words into Phonemes:** (Student can use chopping hand motion to show phonemes.)

Teacher Administration Directions: I will say a word and I will segment the word into the sounds I hear.

Listen. Tube, /t – oo – b/. I hear 3 sounds in tube, /t - oo - b/.

Now it's your turn. The word is "path". What are the sounds you hear in the word "path?"

| | | |
|---|---|---|
| CORRECT RESPONSE: | Yes, when you segment the word path into sounds, you hear /p – ă – th/. |
| INCORRECT RESPONSE: | When I segment the word path into sounds, I hear 3 sounds, /p – ă – th/. Say it back to me: path, /p - ă – th/ |

| | WORD: | CORRECT RESPONSE: | STUDENT RESPONSE: | PLACEMENT SCORE: | STUDENT RESPONSE: | POST SCORE: |
|---|---|---|---|---|---|---|
| 1 | thorn | th – or – n | | | | |
| 2 | switch | s – w – ĭ - tch | | | | |
| 3 | split | s – p – l – ĭ - t | | | | |
| 4 | scooter | s – c – oo – t - er | | | | |
| 5 | claws | c – l – aw - z | | | | |
| 6 | crisp | c - r - i - s - p | | | | |
| | | | Score: /6 | | | |

## PART 3: PHONEME MANIPULATION

**Adding Initial Phonemes:** (Teacher can use hand motion from the curriculum.)

Teacher Administration Directions: I will say a word part. I will add a sound at the beginning to make a new word. Listen, /-ate/. When I add /g/ at the beginning, the word is gate.

Now it's your turn. Say /-oak/. Add /s/ at the beginning and the word is?

| | | | | | | |
|---|---|---|---|---|---|---|
| CORRECT RESPONSE: | Yes, when you add /s/ to /−oak/, the word is soak. | | | | | |
| INCORRECT RESPONSE: | When I add /s/ to /−oak/, the word is soak. Can you say it back to me? /s - oak/, soak. | | | | | |

| | WORD PART: | ADD /*/ AT THE BEGINNING: | CORRECT RESPONSE: | STUDENT RESPONSE: | PLACEMENT SCORE: | STUDENT RESPONSE: | POST SCORE: |
|---|---|---|---|---|---|---|---|
| 1 | /−ox/ | /b/ | box | | | | |
| 2 | /−ice/ | /n/ | nice | | | | |
| 3 | /-air/ | /ch/ | chair | | | | |
| 4 | /-each/ | /r/ | reach | | | | |
| 5 | /−ooth/ | /t/ | tooth | | | | |
| 6 | /-oil/ | /f/ | foil | | | | |
| | | | | Score:      /6 | | | |

**Deleting Initial Phonemes:** (Teacher can use hand motion from the curriculum.)

Teacher Administration Directions: I will say a word. I will delete or take away the first sound and tell you what is left. The word is "shout." Without /sh/, what's left is "out." Now it's your turn. Say, spine. Without /s/, what's left is?

| | | | | | | |
|---|---|---|---|---|---|---|
| CORRECT RESPONSE: | Yes, spine without /s/ is pine. | | | | | |
| INCORRECT RESPONSE: | Let's try again. Say, spine. Without /s/, what's left is pine. Can you say pine? | | | | | |

| | WORD | WITHOUT /*/ | CORRECT RESPONSE: | STUDENT RESPONSE: | PLACEMENT SCORE: | STUDENT RESPONSE: | POST SCORE: |
|---|---|---|---|---|---|---|---|
| 1 | thunder | /th/ | under | | | | |
| 2 | week | /w/ | eek | | | | |
| 3 | told | /t/ | old | | | | |
| 4 | break | /b/ | rake | | | | |
| 5 | slime | /s/ | lime | | | | |
| 6 | flip | /f/ | lip | | | | |
| | | | | Score:      /6 | | | |

**Substituting Initial Phonemes:** (Teacher can use hand motion from the curriculum.)

Teacher Administration Directions: I will say a word. I will change the first sound to make a new word. Listen, the word is best. Change /b/ to /w/ and the word is west.

Now it's your turn. Say nudge. Change /n/ to /j/ and the word is?

| CORRECT RESPONSE: | Yes, when you change /n/ to /j/, the word is judge. |
|---|---|
| INCORRECT RESPONSE: | Let's try it again. Say, nudge. Change /n/ to /j/ and the word is /j/-udge, judge. Can you say judge? |

|  | WORD | CHANGE /*/ TO /*/ | CORRECT RESPONSE: | STUDENT RESPONSE: | PLACEMENT SCORE: | STUDENT RESPONSE: | POST SCORE: |
|---|---|---|---|---|---|---|---|
| 1 | toast | /t/ to /k/ | coast | | | | |
| 2 | change | /ch/ to /r/ | range | | | | |
| 3 | pond | /p/ to /b/ | bond | | | | |
| 4 | slow | /s/ to /g/ | glow | | | | |
| 5 | grade | /g/ to /b/ | braid | | | | |
| 6 | most | /m/ to /h/ | host | | | | |
| | | | | Score: /6 | | | |

*\*\*If a student scores in the 0-3 range for manipulating initial phonemes, end assessment here. Use scoring guide on page 13 to identify where to begin instruction. The remainder of the assessment can be administered once students are proficient at manipulating initial phonemes.\*\**

**Adding Final Phonemes:** (Teacher can use hand motion from the curriculum.)

Teacher Administration Directions: I will say a word. I will add a sound at the end to make a new word. Listen, /bar/. When I add /k/ at the end, the word is bark.

Now it's your turn. Say /shell/. Add /f/ at the end and the word is?

| CORRECT RESPONSE: | Yes, when you add /f/ at the end of /shell/, the word is shelf. |
|---|---|
| INCORRECT RESPONSE: | When I add /f/ to /shell/, the word is /shell/-/f/, shelf. Can you say it back to me? /shell/-/f/, shelf. |

|  | WORD | ADD /*/ AT THE END | CORRECT RESPONSE: | STUDENT RESPONSE: | PLACEMENT SCORE: | STUDENT RESPONSE: | POST SCORE: |
|---|---|---|---|---|---|---|---|
| 1 | stay | /t/ | state | | | | |
| 2 | far | /m/ | farm | | | | |
| 3 | boo | /th/ | booth | | | | |
| 4 | ten | /d/ | tend | | | | |
| 5 | law | /n/ | lawn | | | | |
| 6 | mass | /k/ | mask | | | | |
| | | | | Score: /6 | | | |

## Deleting Final Phonemes: (Teacher can use hand motion from the curriculum.)

Teacher Administration Directions: I will say a word. I will delete or take away the final sound and tell you what is left. The word is "bone." Without /n/, what's left is "bōw." Now it's your turn. Say, grape. Without /p/, what's left is?

| CORRECT RESPONSE: | Yes, grape without /p/ is grey. |
|---|---|
| INCORRECT RESPONSE: | Let's try again. Say, grape. Without /p/, what's left is grey. |

| | WORD | WITHOUT /*/ | CORRECT RESPONSE: | STUDENT RESPONSE: | PLACEMENT SCORE: | STUDENT RESPONSE: | POST SCORE: |
|---|---|---|---|---|---|---|---|
| 1 | torch | /ch/ | tore | | | | |
| 2 | bike | /k/ | by | | | | |
| 3 | plain | /n/ | play | | | | |
| 4 | field | /d/ | feel | | | | |
| 5 | self | /f/ | sell | | | | |
| 6 | grasp | /p/ | grass | | | | |
| | | | | Score: /6 | | | |

## Substituting Final Phonemes: (Teacher can use hand motion from the curriculum.)

Teacher Administration Directions: I will say a word. I will change the last sound to make a new word. Listen, the word is curb. Change /b/ to /v/ and the word is curve. Now it's your turn. Say corn. Change /n/ to /t/ and the word is?

| CORRECT RESPONSE: | Yes, when you change /n/ to /t/, the word is court. |
|---|---|
| INCORRECT RESPONSE: | Let's try it again. Say, corn. Change /n/ to /t/ and the word is /cor/-/t/, court. |

| | WORD | CHANGE /*/ TO /*/ | CORRECT RESPONSE: | STUDENT RESPONSE: | PLACEMENT SCORE: | STUDENT RESPONSE: | POST SCORE: |
|---|---|---|---|---|---|---|---|
| 1 | peak | /k/ to /s/ | peace | | | | |
| 2 | wreath | /th/ to /ch/ | reach | | | | |
| 3 | worse | /s/ to /d/ | word | | | | |
| 4 | bend | /d/ to /t/ | bent | | | | |
| 5 | term | /m/ to /n/ | turn | | | | |
| 6 | sharp | /p/ to /k/ | shark | | | | |
| | | | | Score: /6 | | | |

Substituting Medial Phonemes:

Teacher Administration Directions: I will say a word. I will change the middle or vowel sound to make a new word. Listen, the word is sit. Change /ĭ/ to /ī/ and the word is sight. Now it's your turn.

Say got. Change /ŏ/ to /ō/ and the word is?

| CORRECT RESPONSE: | Yes, when you change /ŏ/ to /ō/, the word is goat. |
|---|---|
| INCORRECT RESPONSE: | Let's try it again. Say, got. Change /ŏ/ to /ō/ and the word is /gō/-/t/, goat. |

| | WORD | CHANGE /*/ TO /*/ | CORRECT RESPONSE: | STUDENT RESPONSE: | PLACEMENT SCORE: | STUDENT RESPONSE: | POST SCORE: |
|---|---|---|---|---|---|---|---|
| 1 | rid | /ĭ/ to /ī/ | ride | | | | |
| 2 | seat | /ē/ to /ĕ/ | set | | | | |
| 3 | mad | /ă/ to /ā/ | made | | | | |
| 4 | net | /ĕ/ to /ō/ | note | | | | |
| 5 | those | /ō/ to /ē/ | these | | | | |
| 6 | bud | /ŭ/ to /ir/ | bird | | | | |
| | | | Score: /6 | | | | |

# Overall Results:

After this assessment has been given, use this section to record anecdotal notes about the student's strengths and areas of need. This can be especially helpful when planning for intervention.

Areas of Strength:

Areas of Need & Plan for Intervention:

# Scoring Guidelines for Bridge the Gap Placement Assessment:

Teachers: Record student scores from the placement assessment to identify where to begin instruction.

The skills that have a score below 80% (0-4 correct responses) would be the specific skills that can be targeted for instruction when using Bridge the Gap.

| PHONEME ISOLATION | | | | PART 1 |
|---|---|---|---|---|
| PHONEMIC AWARENESS SKILL | TOTAL | PLACEMENT SCORE | POST SCORE | BRIDGE THE GAP |
| Initial Sounds | 6 | | | Lessons 1-12 |
| Final Sounds | 6 | | | Lessons 13-24 |
| Medial Sounds | 6 | | | Lessons 25-36 |
| BLENDING & SEGMENTING | | | | PART 2 |
| PHONEMIC AWARENESS SKILL | TOTAL | PLACEMENT SCORE | POST SCORE | BRIDGE THE GAP |
| Blending Syllables | 6 | | | Lessons 1-10 |
| Segmenting into Syllables | 6 | | | Lessons 1-10 |
| Blending Phonemes | 6 | | | Lessons 11 - 25 |
| Segmenting Words into Phonemes | 6 | | | Lessons 11 - 25 |
| PHONEME MANIPULATION | | | | PART 3 |
| PHONEMIC AWARENESS SKILL | TOTAL | PLACEMENT SCORE | POST SCORE | BRIDGE THE GAP |
| Adding Initial Phonemes | 6 | | | Lessons 1-10 |
| Deleting Initial Phonemes | 6 | | | Lessons 1-10 |
| Substituting Initial Phonemes | 6 | | | Lessons 29-38 |
| Adding Final Phonemes | 6 | | | Lessons 11-20 |
| Deleting Final Phonemes | 6 | | | Lessons 11-20 |
| Substituting Final Phonemes | 6 | | | Lessons 39-48 |
| Substituting Medial Phonemes | 6 | | | Lessons 49-58 |

Note: Adding & Deleting with Consonant Blends are included in Lessons 21-28, however they are not assessed in this initial assessment.

Substituting Various Phonemes activities are included in Lessons 59-70.

# Bridge the Gap

HEGGERTY PHONEMIC AWARENESS
INTERVENTION LESSONS

2020 EDITION

by Alisa VanHekken and
Marjorie Bottari

# Bridge the Gap: Table of Contents

# Phoneme Isolation

# Defining Terms

Teachers can use the definitions to explain the skill and set the purpose for the lesson.

### 1. Phoneme:

A phoneme is the smallest unit of sound.

### 2. Isolate:

When we isolate a sound, we identify one sound and say it by itself. We can isolate a sound at the beginning of a word, at the end of a word, or in the middle of a word.

### 3. Initial Sound:

The initial sound is the first sound we hear in a word. The initial sound can be a consonant, vowel, or the first sound of a consonant blend.

### 4. Final Sound:

The final sound is the last sound we hear in a word. We can also define it as the sound at the end of a word.

### 5. Medial Sound:

The medial sound is the sound in the middle of the word. It is the vowel sound in the words we will say aloud. Every word needs a vowel sound.

*Note: Teacher can choose to use the term medial or vowel sound during instruction.*

---

Teachers can scaffold support using hand motions.

✋

## HAND MOTIONS

**ROLLER COASTER HAND MOTION FOR ISOLATING MEDIAL SOUNDS**

Teacher and students move their arm like a roller coaster going over a hill. The bottom of the hill is the beginning of the word, top of the hill is the medial/vowel sound, and bottom of the hill is the end of the word.

**PUNCH IT OUT HAND MOTION FOR ISOLATING FINAL SOUNDS**

The teacher models the "punch it out" hand motion using his or her left arm. Slide your forearm across your body when saying the first part of the word and punch straight up into the air when saying the final sound.

---

# Anchor Lesson: Initial Phoneme Isolation

LESSON FOCUS: Words are made up of individual sounds. The initial phoneme is the first sound we hear in a word. In these lessons, we will say a word and isolate the first sound we hear.

## I DO:

The first or intial sound is what we hear at the beginning of a word.

I will say a word and isolate the first (initial) sound I hear.

| big | T: The first sound we hear in the word big is /b/. /b/, big. Can you say that?<br><br>S: /b/, big |
| --- | --- |
| road | T: The first sound we hear in the word road is /r/. /r/, road. Can you say that?<br><br>S: /r/, road |

## WE DO:

Let's try some words together. I will say a word. We will repeat the word and isolate the first sound we hear.

| jump | T: Say, jump<br><br>T & S: jump<br><br>T: What is the first sound we hear in jump?<br><br>T & S: /j/ |
| --- | --- |
| field | T: Say, field<br><br>T & S: field<br><br>T: What is the first sound we hear in field?<br><br>T & S: /f/ |

## YOU DO:

Now it's your turn. I will say a word, you will repeat the word and isolate the first sound you hear.

| noise | T: Say, noise<br><br>S: noise, /n/ |
| --- | --- |
| pail | T: Say, pail<br><br>S: pail, /p/ |

### TEACHER TIPS:

1. Anchor the sounds to a visual: Use colored tiles, felt squares or chips to represent the initial, medial, and final sound in a word.

   *Example:* ■ ■ ■    *In this example, the first square is the first sound; second square is the medial sound; third square is the final sound.*

   This visual can be used by the teacher or given to the students.

   The first square (initial sound) would be touched when saying the first sound in a word that is spoken aloud.

2. Demonstrate what the terms initial, final and medial mean by asking 3 students to line up. The first person in the line is the initial sound in a word, the last person in line is the final sound in a word, and the second person in line is the medial sound in a word. 3 small figures in a line can also be used to demonstrate initial, final and medial positions.

# Initial Phoneme Isolation

LESSON FOCUS: The initial phoneme is the first sound we hear in a word. In these lessons, you will say a word and isolate the first sound you hear.

Teacher Directions: I will say a word. You will repeat the word and isolate the first sound you hear.

### ⇨ Lesson 1:

| WORD | INITIAL SOUND |
|------|---------------|
| done | /d/ |
| find | /f/ |
| match | /m/ |
| take | /t/ |
| park | /p/ |

### ⇨ Lesson 2:

| WORD | INITIAL SOUND |
|------|---------------|
| people | /p/ |
| headphones | /h/ |
| super | /s/ |
| mindful | /m/ |
| ribbon | /r/ |

### ⇨ Lesson 3:

| WORD | INITIAL SOUND |
|------|---------------|
| turtle | /t/ |
| kitchen | /k/ |
| review | /r/ |
| dollar | /d/ |
| cookies | /k/ |

### ⇨ Lesson 4:

| WORD | INITIAL SOUND |
|------|---------------|
| guitar | /g/ |
| color | /k/ |
| zipper | /z/ |
| letters | /l/ |
| partner | /p/ |

### ⇨ Lesson 5:

| WORD | INITIAL SOUND |
|------|---------------|
| actual | /ă/ |
| hunger | /h/ |
| opposite | /ŏ/ |
| dialogue | /d/ |
| century | /s/ |

### ⇨ Lesson 6:

| WORD | INITIAL SOUND |
|------|---------------|
| eager | /ē/ |
| matter | /m/ |
| whisper | /wh/ |
| central | /s/ |
| shoulder | /sh/ |

# Initial Phoneme Isolation

LESSON FOCUS: The initial phoneme is the first sound we hear in a word. In these lessons, you will say a word and isolate the first sound you hear.

Teacher Directions: I will say a word. You will repeat the word and isolate the first sound you hear.

Lesson 7:

| WORD | INITIAL SOUND |
|------|---------------|
| atlas | /ă/ |
| solar | /s/ |
| family | /f/ |
| icing | /ī/ |
| volcano | /v/ |

Lesson 8:

| WORD | INITIAL SOUND |
|------|---------------|
| noodles | /n/ |
| ocean | /ō/ |
| symbol | /s/ |
| waffle | /w/ |
| position | /p/ |

Lesson 9:

| WORD | INITIAL SOUND |
|------|---------------|
| dependent | /d/ |
| combine | /k/ |
| octagon | /ŏ/ |
| universe | /ū/ |
| repair | /r/ |

Lesson 10:

| WORD | INITIAL SOUND |
|------|---------------|
| between | /b/ |
| organize | /or/ |
| everything | /ĕ/ |
| upstairs | /ŭ/ |
| thousand | /th/ |

Lesson 11:

| WORD | INITIAL SOUND |
|------|---------------|
| zebra | /z/ |
| shopping | /sh/ |
| apron | /ā/ |
| wonder | /w/ |
| itchy | /ĭ/ |

Lesson 12:

| WORD | INITIAL SOUND |
|------|---------------|
| yellow | /y/ |
| laughter | /l/ |
| icing | /ī/ |
| chicken | /ch/ |
| actor | /ă/ |

# Anchor Lesson: Final Phoneme Isolation

LESSON FOCUS: Words are made up of individual sounds. In these lessons, we will say a word and isolate the final or last sound we hear.

## I DO:

The final or last sound in a word is what we hear at the end of a word.

I will say a word and isolate the final (last) sound I hear.

| look | T: The last sound we hear in the word look is /k/. Look, /k/ Can you say that?<br><br>S: look, /k/ |
|------|--------------------------------------------------------------------------------------|
| rope | T: The last sound we hear in the word rope is /p/. Rope /p/. Can you say that?<br><br>S: rope, /p/ |

## WE DO:

Let's try some words together. I will say the word. We will repeat the word and isolate the final sound we hear.

| knob | T: Say, knob<br><br>T & S: knob<br><br>T: What is the final sound we hear in knob?<br><br>T & S: /b/ |
|-------|-------------------------------------------------------------------------------------|
| sweet | T: Say, sweet<br><br>T & S: sweet<br><br>T: What is the final sound we hear in sweet?<br><br>T & S: /t/ |

## YOU DO:

Now it's your turn. I will say a word. You will repeat the word and isolate the final sound you hear.

| swim | T: Say, swim<br><br>S: swim, /m/ |
|------|----------------------------------|
| love | T: Say, love<br><br>S: love, /v/ |

SCAFFOLD SUPPORT WITH HAND MOTION:

The teacher models the "punch it out" hand motion using his or her left arm. Slide your forearm across your body when saying the first part of the word and punch straight up into the air when saying the final sound.

### TEACHER TIPS:

1. Anchor the sounds to a visual: Use colored tiles, felt squares or chips to represent the initial, medial, and final sound in a word.

   Example: ■ ■ ■   *In this example, the first square is the first sound; second square is the medial sound; third square is the final sound.*

   The last square is the final sound. Teachers and students can touch the last square when isolating the final sound.

2. Demonstrate what the words last or final mean by asking 3 students to line up. The last person in line is like the final/last sound in a word. Or use 3 small figures in a line to demonstrate last.

# Final Phoneme Isolation

LESSON FOCUS: The final sound is the last sound we hear in a word. In these lessons, you will say a word and isolate the final or last sound you hear.

Teacher Directions: I will say a word. You will repeat the word and then isolate the final (last) sound you hear in the word.

⇨ Lesson 13:

| WORD | FINAL SOUND |
|------|-------------|
| steam | /m/ |
| plug | /g/ |
| squeak | /k/ |
| plant | /t/ |
| bend | /d/ |

⇨ Lesson 14:

| WORD | FINAL SOUND |
|------|-------------|
| outside | /d/ |
| watch | /ch/ |
| popcorn | /n/ |
| wrote | /t/ |
| spaceship | /p/ |

⇨ Lesson 15:

| WORD | FINAL SOUND |
|------|-------------|
| erase | /s/ |
| headlight | /t/ |
| wildlife | /f/ |
| notebook | /k/ |
| goldfish | /sh/ |

⇨ Lesson 16:

| WORD | FINAL SOUND |
|------|-------------|
| around | /d/ |
| begin | /n/ |
| panic | /k/ |
| moment | /t/ |
| fireplace | /s/ |

⇨ Lesson 17:

| WORD | FINAL SOUND |
|------|-------------|
| redeem | /m/ |
| beside | /d/ |
| import | /t/ |
| eclipse | /s/ |
| body | /ē/ |

⇨ Lesson 18:

| WORD | FINAL SOUND |
|------|-------------|
| absent | /t/ |
| between | /n/ |
| police | /s/ |
| drafty | /ē/ |
| compound | /d/ |

✋ SCAFFOLD SUPPORT WITH HAND MOTION:

The teacher models the "punch it out" hand motion using his or her left arm. Slide your forearm across your body when saying the first part of the word and punch straight up into the air when saying the final sound.

# Final Phoneme Isolation

LESSON FOCUS: The final sound is the last sound we hear in a word. In these lessons, you will say a word and isolate the final or last sound you hear.

Teacher Directions: I will say a word. You will repeat the word and then isolate the final (last) sound you hear in the word.

⇨ Lesson 19:

| WORD | FINAL SOUND |
|------|-------------|
| giraffe | /f/ |
| squeeze | /z/ |
| balloon | /n/ |
| depart | /t/ |
| panic | /k/ |

⇨ Lesson 20:

| WORD | FINAL SOUND |
|------|-------------|
| disturb | /b/ |
| window | /ō/ |
| stories | /z/ |
| system | /m/ |
| waited | /d/ |

⇨ Lesson 21:

| WORD | FINAL SOUND |
|------|-------------|
| thought | /t/ |
| country | /ē/ |
| exchange | /j/ |
| because | /z/ |
| mountain | /n/ |

⇨ Lesson 22:

| WORD | FINAL SOUND |
|------|-------------|
| offense | /s/ |
| engage | /j/ |
| against | /t/ |
| harmony | /ē/ |
| unpack | /k/ |

⇨ Lesson 23:

| WORD | FINAL SOUND |
|------|-------------|
| rejoice | /s/ |
| sandwich | /ch/ |
| destroy | /oy/ |
| browse | /z/ |
| shower | /er/ |

⇨ Lesson 24:

| WORD | FINAL SOUND |
|------|-------------|
| expensive | /v/ |
| simplify | /ī/ |
| hollow | /ō/ |
| photograph | /f/ |
| beneath | /th/ |

✋ SCAFFOLD SUPPORT WITH HAND MOTION:

The teacher models the "punch it out" hand motion using his or her left arm. Slide your forearm across your body when saying the first part of the word and punch straight up into the air when saying the final sound.

# Anchor Lesson: Medial Phoneme Isolation

LESSON FOCUS: Words are made up of individual sounds. Today we will work with words that have 3 sounds. We will isolate the medial or vowel sound we here in these words. Remember every word has a vowel sound in it.

### I DO:

When we hear three sounds in a word, the vowel sound is the sound we hear in the middle of the word.

I will say a word and isolate the medial (vowel) sound I hear.

| bake | T: Bake. We hear three sounds in bake: /b/ - /ā/ - /k/. The vowel sound we hear in the middle of the word bake is /ā/. Can you say bake, /ā/? S: Bake, /ā/ |
|------|------|
| top | T: Top. We hear three sounds in top: /t/ /ŏ/ /p/. The vowel sound we hear in the middle is /ŏ/. Can you say top, /ŏ/? S: Top, /ŏ/ |

### WE DO:

Let's try some words together. I will say the word. We will repeat the word and isolate the vowel sound we hear.

| soap | T: Say, soap  T & S: soap  T: What is the vowel sound we hear in soap?  T & S: /ō/ |
|------|------|
| neck | T: Say, neck  T & S: neck  T: What is the vowel sound we hear in neck?  T & S: /ĕ/ |

### YOU DO:

Now it is your turn. I will say a word. You will repeat the word and isolate the vowel sound you hear in the middle of the word.

| mice | T: Say, mice  S: mice, /ī/ |
|------|------|
| sun | T: Say, sun  S: sun, /ŭ/ |

**SCAFFOLD SUPPORT WITH HAND MOTION:**

Teacher and students move their arm like a roller coaster going over a hill. The bottom of the hill is the beginning of the word, top of the hill is the medial/vowel sound, and bottom of the hill is the end of the word.

## TEACHER TIPS:

1. Anchor the sounds to a visual: Use colored tiles, felt squares or chips to represent the initial, medial, and final sound in a word.

   Example: ■ ■ ■   *In this example, the first square is the first sound; second square is the medial sound; third square is the final sound.*

   This visual can be used by the teacher or given to the students. This visual can be used by the teacher or given to the students. Teachers and students can touch the second square when isolating the medial or vowel sound in a word that is spoken aloud.

2. Demonstrate what the words *middle* or *medial* means by asking 3 students to line up. The second person in line is like the middle sound in a word. Or use 3 small figures in a line to demonstrate where the middle is.

3. If students need to review vowel sounds, use vowel flashcards to review the sounds of the vowels: a, i, o, u, e, y, and r-controlled and advanced vowel sounds.

# Medial Phoneme Isolation

LESSON FOCUS: The medial or vowel sound is the sound we hear in the middle of a word. Remember, every word has a vowel sound in it.  We will hear words with short or long vowel sounds in the middle.

Teacher Directions: I will say a word. You will repeat the word and then isolate the vowel sound you hear in the middle of the word.

⊙ Lesson 25:

| WORD | MEDIAL SOUND |
|------|--------------|
| feed | /ē/ |
| got | /ŏ/ |
| rake | /ā/ |
| bite | /ī/ |
| cut | /ŭ/ |

⊙ Lesson 26:

| WORD | MEDIAL SOUND |
|------|--------------|
| sick | /ĭ/ |
| road | /ō/ |
| beach | /ē/ |
| pack | /ă/ |
| set | /ĕ/ |

⊙ Lesson 27:

| WORD | MEDIAL SOUND |
|------|--------------|
| fetch | /ĕ/ |
| grasp | /ă/ |
| toast | /ō/ |
| claim | /ā/ |
| plus | /ŭ/ |

⊙ Lesson 28:

| WORD | MEDIAL SOUND |
|------|--------------|
| crisp | /ĭ/ |
| green | /ē/ |
| brave | /ā/ |
| glide | /ī/ |
| flop | /ŏ/ |

✋ ROLLER COASTER HAND MOTION:

Teacher and students move their arm like a roller coaster going over a hill.  The bottom of the hill is the beginning of the word, top of the hill is the medial/vowel sound, and bottom of the hill is the end of the word.

*You may choose to use vowel flashcards to review the vowel sounds*

# Medial Phoneme Isolation

LESSON FOCUS: The medial sound or vowel sound is the sound we hear in the middle of a word. We will hear words with advanced vowel sounds in the middle. Advanced vowels can be r-controlled vowel sounds, such as /er/, /or/, /are/ or sounds like /oo/, /oi/ and /aw/.

Teacher Directions: I will say a word. You will repeat the word and then isolate the vowel sound you hear in the middle of the word.

⊕ Lesson 29:

| WORD | MEDIAL SOUND |
|------|-------------|
| born | /or/ |
| dirt | /ir/ |
| join | /oi/ |
| cause | /au/ |
| loud | /ou/ |

⊕ Lesson 30:

| WORD | MEDIAL SOUND |
|------|-------------|
| void | /oi/ |
| curve | /ur/ |
| mouse | /ou/ |
| yawn | /aw/ |
| food | /oo/ |

⊕ Lesson 31:

| WORD | MEDIAL SOUND |
|------|-------------|
| hoop | /oo/ |
| shout | /ou/ |
| hard | /ar/ |
| coin | /oi/ |
| yawn | /aw/ |

⊕ Lesson 32:

| WORD | MEDIAL SOUND |
|------|-------------|
| soon | /oo/ |
| herd | /er/ |
| dawn | /aw/ |
| farm | /ar/ |
| coil | /oi/ |

🖐 ROLLER COASTER HAND MOTION:

Teacher and students move their arm like a roller coaster going over a hill. The bottom of the hill is the beginning of the word, top of the hill is the medial/vowel sound, and bottom of the hill is the end of the word.

*You may choose to use vowel flashcards to review the vowel sounds. Letters are **; Sound(s) is/are /*/.*

🍎

### TEACHER TIP:

Anchor the sounds to a visual: Use colored tiles, felt squares or chips to represent the initial, medial, and final sound in a word.

*Example:* ■ ■ ■   *In this example, the first square is the first sound; second square is the medial sound; third square is the final sound.*

This visual can be used by the teacher or given to the students. Teachers and students can touch the second square when isolating the medial or vowel sound in a word that is spoken aloud.

# Medial Phoneme Isolation

LESSON FOCUS: The medial or vowel sound is the sound we hear in the middle of a word. We will continue to isolate the medial or vowel sounds in words. We will hear words with short, long, and advanced vowel sounds.

Teacher Directions: I will say a word. You will repeat the word and then isolate the vowel sound you hear in the middle of the word.

**Lesson 33:**

| WORD | MEDIAL SOUND |
|------|--------------|
| tooth | /oo/ |
| north | /or/ |
| noise | /oi/ |
| shirt | /ir/ |
| lawn | /aw/ |

**Lesson 34:**

| WORD | MEDIAL SOUND |
|------|--------------|
| large | /ar/ |
| chalk | /aw/ |
| shook | /oo/ |
| sort | /or/ |
| this | /ĭ/ |

**Lesson 35:**

| WORD | MEDIAL SOUND |
|------|--------------|
| wait | /ā/ |
| chart | /ar/ |
| thorn | /or/ |
| boot | /oo/ |
| sauce | /au/ |

**Lesson 36:**

| WORD | MEDIAL SOUND |
|------|--------------|
| cause | /au/ |
| pork | /or/ |
| join | /oi/ |
| seem | /ē/ |
| foot | /oo/ |

**ROLLER COASTER HAND MOTION:**

Teacher and students move their arm like a roller coaster going over a hill. The bottom of the hill is the beginning of the word, top of the hill is the medial/vowel sound, and bottom of the hill is the end of the word.

*You may choose to use vowel flashcards to review the vowel sounds*

# Phoneme Isolation

LESSON FOCUS: We have spent some lessons listening for the beginning, medial/vowel and final sounds. In our next few lessons, we will isolate all of the sounds we hear in the word.

Teacher says, "I will say a word and I will isolate the first sound, the medial/vowel sound, and the final sound. The word is bake. The first sound is /b/; the medial/vowel sound is /ā/; and the final sound is /k/."

| WORD | FIRST SOUND | MEDIAL SOUND | FINAL SOUND |
|------|-------------|--------------|-------------|
| bake | /b/ | /ā/ | /k/ |

## Lesson 37:

Teacher Directions: I will say a word and ask you to isolate the first sound, the medial/vowel sound, and the final sound.

Student Response:  Student repeats the word and isolates the indicated sound.

Teacher: What is the first sound? What is the medial/vowel sound?  What is the final sound?

| WORD | FIRST SOUND | MEDIAL SOUND | FINAL SOUND |
|------|-------------|--------------|-------------|
| top | /t/ | /ŏ/ | /p/ |
| paid | /p/ | /ā/ | /d/ |
| jet | /j/ | /ĕ/ | /t/ |
| wish | /w/ | /ĭ/ | /sh/ |
| back | /b/ | /ă/ | /k/ |

## Lesson 38: Phoneme Isolation

Teacher Directions: I will say a word and ask you to isolate the first sound, the medial/vowel sound, and the final sound.

Student Response:  Student repeats the word and isolates the indicated sound.

Teacher: What is the first sound? What is the medial/vowel sound?  What is the final sound?

| WORD | FIRST SOUND | MEDIAL SOUND | FINAL SOUND |
|------|-------------|--------------|-------------|
| dig | /d/ | /ĭ/ | /g/ |
| hum | /h/ | /ŭ/ | /m/ |
| lake | /l/ | /ā/ | /k/ |
| side | /s/ | /ī/ | /d/ |
| cute | /k/ | /ū/ | /t/ |

### TEACHER TIP:

Use a colored square (felt sqares, magnetic tiles, counters, cubes, or chips) to provide a visual anchor for the sounds. Each square represents a sound. Teacher and/or students touch each cube, counter or tile when saying each sound aloud.

# Phoneme Isolation

LESSON FOCUS: We will continue listening to words with 3 sounds. We will isolate the beginning, medial/vowel and final sounds in the words we hear.

⊜ Lesson 39: Phoneme Isolation

Teacher Directions: I will say a word and ask you to isolate the first sound, the medial/vowel sound, and the final sound.

Student Response:  Student repeats the word and isolates the indicated sound.

Teacher: What is the first sound? What is the medial/vowel sound?  What is the final sound?

| WORD | FIRST SOUND | MEDIAL SOUND | FINAL SOUND |
|------|-------------|--------------|-------------|
| word | /w/ | /er/ | /d/ |
| chart | /ch/ | /ar/ | /t/ |
| house | /h/ | /ou/ | /s/ |
| coin | /k/ | /oi/ | /n/ |
| fork | /f/ | /or/ | /k/ |

⊜ Lesson 40: Phoneme Isolation

Teacher Directions: I will say a word and ask you to isolate the first sound, the medial/vowel sound, and the final sound.

Student Response:  Student repeats the word and isolates the indicated sound.

Teacher: What is the first sound? What is the medial/vowel sound?  What is the final sound?

| WORD | FIRST SOUND | MEDIAL SOUND | FINAL SOUND |
|------|-------------|--------------|-------------|
| caught | /k/ | /au/ | /t/ |
| good | /g/ | /oo/ | /d/ |
| down | /d/ | /ow/ | /n/ |
| farm | /f/ | /ar/ | /m/ |
| loop | /l/ | /oo/ | /p/ |

### TEACHER TIP:

Use a colored square (felt sqares, magnetic tiles, counters, cubes, or chips) to provide a visual anchor for the sounds. Each square represents a sound. Teacher and/or students touch each cube, counter or tile when saying each sound aloud.

✎ CONNECT TO PRINT (PHONICS):

Ask the students to write a letter(s) to match each sound on a dry erase board.

# Phoneme Isolation

We have been listening to words with three sounds. We have isolated the beginning, medial/vowel and final sounds in the words we hear. Today, you are going to show me what you learned.

Teacher Directions: I will say a word, you will say the word back to me. I will ask you to isolate the first sound, medial (vowel) sound, and the final sound you hear in the word.

Recording Directions: Record incorrect responses in the Student Response column. If correct, mark with a check or +

Student Name: _____     Date: _____

|  | WHOLE WORD | INITIAL SOUND | STUDENT RESPONSE (INITIAL) | MEDIAL SOUND | STUDENT RESPONSE (MEDIAL) | FINAL SOUND | STUDENT RESPONSE (FINAL) |
|---|---|---|---|---|---|---|---|
| 1 | mood | /m/ | | /oo/ | | /d/ | |
| 2 | sort | /s/ | | /or/ | | /t/ | |
| 3 | tap | /t/ | | /ă/ | | /p/ | |
| 4 | noise | /n/ | | /oi/ | | /z/ | |
| 5 | couch | /k/ | | /ou/ | | /ch/ | |
| 6 | part | /p/ | | /ar/ | | /t/ | |
| 7 | his | /h/ | | /ĭ/ | | /z/ | |
| 8 | choice | /ch/ | | /oi/ | | /s/ | |
| 9 | dawn | /d/ | | /aw/ | | /n/ | |
| 10 | shout | /sh/ | | /ou/ | | /t/ | |
| | | | /10 | | /10 | | /10 |

## SCORING GUIDE:

**Initial Sound**

0-5 correct: Review Initial Phoneme Isolation Lessons 1-12

6-8 correct: Review Initial Phoneme Isolation Lessons 6-12

9-10 correct: Provide instruction in isolating medial or final sounds if needed or move on to Part 2 (Blending & Segmenting).

**Final Sound**

0-5 correct: Review Final Phoneme Isolation Lessons 13-24

6-8 correct: Review Final Phoneme Isolation Lessons 19-24

9-10 correct: Provide instruction in isolating intial sounds or medial if needed or move on to Part 2 (Blending & Segmenting).

**Medial (Vowel) Sound**

0-5 correct: Review Medial Phoneme Isolation Lessons 25-36

6-8 correct: Review Medial Phoneme Isolation Lessons 31-36

9-10 correct: Provide instruction in isolating initial or final sounds if needed or move on to Part 2 (Blending & Segmenting).

PART 2

# Blending & Segmenting

# Defining Terms

Teachers can use the definitions to explain the skill and set the purpose for the lesson.

### 1. Blending

A phonological awareness skill where the parts of a word are blended into a whole word. The teacher provides the parts of a word and the student blend or "say it fast" into a spoken word. In our lessons, these parts can be syllables or phonemes/sounds the students hear aloud. This is a skill that we work on orally during the phonemic awareness lesson, and it transfers into reading and print when students decode or read words.

### 2. Segmenting

A phonological awareness skill where the teacher says a whole word and students separate or segment the word into syllables or phonemes/sounds. This is a skill we work on orally in the phonemic awareness lesson, and it transfers to print as students write and spell words (encoding).

### 3. Syllable

A syllable is a word part with a working vowel sound in it. Words may have 1 syllable, 2 syllables, 3 syllables, and long words can have 4, 5, or 6 syllables.

### 4. Phoneme

A phoneme is the smallest unit of sound. In the lessons, students will blend phonemes into a word, and segment a word into individual phonemes. A phoneme can also be called a sound.

---

## Teachers can scaffold support using hand motions.

✋

### HAND MOTIONS

**BLENDING HAND MOTION:**

Place palms together (or one hand can be used). The teacher chops hands from right to left, one chop for each syllable/phoneme. Then slide hands right to left to say the whole word. Student mirrors the teacher.

**SEGMENTING HAND MOTION:**

Use hands in a chopping motion to represent the syllable/phoneme; one chop for each syllable/phoneme. Finger tapping for each syllable/phoneme can also be used.

---

# Anchor Lesson: Blending Syllables into Words

LESSON FOCUS: When we blend, we put parts of a word together to make a whole word. In these lessons, we will blend syllables into a whole word.

## I DO:

When I say two syllables, I can blend the syllables (or say them fast) to make a whole word:

| num-ber<br>number | T: Watch me. When I blend the two syllables num - ber, the word is number.<br><br>Listen: num - ber, number. |
|---|---|
| un - til<br>until | T: Watch me. When I blend the two syllables un - til, the word is until.<br><br>Listen: un - til, until. |

## WE DO:

Let's try a word together. I will say the syllables. We will repeat the syllables and blend them together into a whole word.

| part - ner<br>partner | T: Repeat after me: part - ner<br><br>T & S: part - ner<br><br>T: What's the word?<br><br>T & S: partner |
|---|---|
| com-plete<br>complete | T: Repeat after me: com - plete<br><br>T & S: com - plete<br><br>T: What's the word?<br><br>T & S: complete |

## YOU DO:

I will say the syllables. You will repeat the syllables and blend them into a whole word. *Students can immediately blend the syllables into the word without repeating.*

| un - der<br>under | T: un-der<br>S: un-der, under |
|---|---|
| dis - cuss<br>discuss | T: dis-cuss<br>S: dis-cuss, discuss |
| el - bow<br>elbow | T: el-bow<br>S: el-bow, elbow |
| sim - pli -fy<br>simplify | T: sim-pli-fy<br>S: sim-pli-fy, simplify |

**BLENDING HAND MOTION:**

Place palms together (or one hand can be used). The teacher chops hands from right to left, one chop for each syllable. Then slide hands right to left to say the whole word. Student mirrors the teacher.

**TEACHER TIP:**

Use a colored square (felt squares, magnetic tiles, counters, cubes, or chips) to anchor the syllables for students. Each square represents a syllable.

# Anchor Lesson: Segmenting Words into Syllables

LESSON FOCUS: When we segment, we say a whole word and separate the word into the syllables we hear. In these lessons, we will segment words into the syllables we hear.

### I DO:

I will say a word and then segment it into the syllables I hear.

| winter | T: Watch me. The word is winter. When I segment the word winter, I hear two syllables: win - ter. |
|---|---|
| flavor | T: Watch me. The word is flavor. When I segment flavor, I hear two syllables: fla - vor. |

### WE DO:

Let's try some words together. I will say the word. You will repeat the word and segment it into the syllables you hear.

| reading | T: Say, reading. <br> T & S: reading <br> T: Segment reading into the syllables you hear. <br> T & S: read - ing |
|---|---|
| basket | T: Say, basket <br> T & S: basket <br> T: Segment basket into the syllables you hear. <br> T & S: bas - kit |

### YOU DO:

I will say a word. You will repeat the word and segment it into the syllables you hear.

| sister | T: sister <br> S: sister, sis-ter |
|---|---|
| pencil | T: pencil <br> S: pencil, pen-cil |
| window | T: window <br> S: window, win-dow |
| powerful | T: powerful <br> S: powerful, pow-er-ful |

---

**SEGMENTING HAND MOTION:**

Use hands in a chopping motion to represent the syllables; one chop for each syllable. Finger tapping for each syllable can also be used.

---

**TEACHER TIP:**

Use a colored square (felt squares, magnetic tiles, counters, cubes, or chips) to anchor the syllables for students. Each square represents a syllable.

# Blending Syllables

LESSON FOCUS: When we blend, we put parts of a word together to make a whole word.

⟳ Blending Lesson 1: Blending Syllables into a Word

Teacher Directions: I will say two syllables, and you will blend the syllables into a word.

Student Response options:

1. Student repeats the syllables aloud and blends the syllables into a whole word.

2. Student hears the syllables and immediately blends the syllables into a whole word.

| SYLLABLES | CORRECT RESPONSE |
|-----------|------------------|
| ab - sent | absent |
| dis - play | display |
| ad - mit | admit |

| SYLLABLES | CORRECT RESPONSE |
|-----------|------------------|
| im - pact | impact |
| en - ter | enter |
| hab - it | habit |

✋ BLENDING HAND MOTION: Place palms together (or one hand can be used). The teacher chops hands from right to left, one chop for each syllable. Then slide hands right to left to say the whole word. Student mirrors the teacher.

🍎 TEACHER TIP: Provide the number of syllables to blend: "Blend the 2 syllables, ab - sent, into a whole word."

# Segmenting into Syllables

LESSON FOCUS: When we segment, we say a whole word and separate the word into the syllables we hear.

⟳ Segmenting Lesson 1: Segmenting Words into 2 Syllables

Teacher Directions: I will say the whole word. You will repeat the word and segment it into the syllables you hear.

Student Response: Student repeats the word aloud and segments the word into syllables.

| WHOLE WORD | CORRECT RESPONSE |
|------------|------------------|
| empty | emp - ty |
| finger | fing - er |
| involve | in - volve |

| WHOLE WORD | CORRECT RESPONSE |
|------------|------------------|
| finish | fin - ish |
| simple | sim - ple |
| rescue | res - cue |

✋ SEGMENTING HAND MOTION: Use hands in a chopping motion to represent the syllables; one chop for each syllable. Finger tapping for each syllable can also be used.

🍎 TEACHER TIP: Provide the number of syllables to segment: "Tell me the 2 syllables in the word empty."

# Blending Syllables

LESSON FOCUS: When we blend, we put parts of a word together to make a whole word.

⇨ Blending Lesson 2: Blending 2 Syllables into a Word

Teacher Directions: I will say two syllables, and you will blend the syllables into a word.

Student Response options:

1. Student repeats the syllables aloud and blends the syllables into a whole word.

2. Student hears the syllables and immediately blends the syllables into a whole word.

| SYLLABLES | CORRECT RESPONSE |
|---|---|
| ĭn - vīte | invite |
| căn - dle | candle |
| hăb - ĭt | habit |

| SYLLABLES | CORRECT RESPONSE |
|---|---|
| shăd - ow | shadow |
| flĭck - er | flicker |
| ĕn - ter | enter |

✋ BLENDING HAND MOTION: Place palms together (or one hand can be used). The teacher chops hands from right to left, one chop for each syllable. Then slide hands right to left to say the whole word. Student mirrors the teacher.

🍎 TEACHER TIP: Provide the number of syllables to blend: "Blend the 2 syllables, in - vite, into a whole word."

# Segmenting into Syllables

LESSON FOCUS: When we segment, we say a whole word and separate the word into the syllables we hear.

⇨ Segmenting Lesson 2: Segmenting Words into 2 Syllables

Teacher Directions: I will say the whole word. You will repeat the word and segment it into the syllables you hear.

Student Response: Student repeats the word aloud and segments the word into syllables.

| WHOLE WORD | CORRECT RESPONSE |
|---|---|
| lately | lāte - ly |
| power | pow - er |
| until | ŭn - til |

| WHOLE WORD | CORRECT RESPONSE |
|---|---|
| whisper | whĭs - per |
| planet | plăn - ĭt |
| recess | rē - cĕss |

✋ SEGMENTING HAND MOTION: Use hands in a chopping motion to represent the syllables; one chop for each syllable. Finger tapping for each syllable can also be used.

🍎 TEACHER TIP: Provide index cards, felt squares or chips to represent the 2 syllables.

# Blending Syllables

🍎 **TEACHER TIP:** Call attention to the shift in the number of syllables you will be blending. "We have been blending two syllables to make a word. Today, we are going to hear words that have 3 syllables. You are going to blend those syllables together to make a whole word. Watch me, "cal-en-der, calendar. You try it. Say cal-en-der (student repeats), what's the word? (calendar)."

**LESSON FOCUS:** When we blend, we put parts of a word together to make a whole word.

⇨ Blending Lesson 3: Blending 3 Syllables into a Word

Teacher Directions: I will say the syllables, and you will blend the syllables into a word.

Student Response options:

1. Student repeats the syllables aloud and blends the syllables into a whole word.

2. Student hears the syllables and immediately blends the syllables into a whole word.

| SYLLABLES | CORRECT RESPONSE |
|---|---|
| tor - nā - dō | tornado |
| rē - turn - ing | returning |
| cŭn - tĕnt - mĭnt | contentment |

| SYLLABLES | CORRECT RESPONSE |
|---|---|
| dĕd - ĭ - cāte | dedicate |
| part - ner - shĭp | partnership |
| nĕg - ŭ - tĭv | negative |

✋ **BLENDING HAND MOTION:** Place palms together (or one hand can be used). The teacher chops hands from right to left, one chop for each syllable. Then slide hands right to left to say the whole word. Student mirrors the teacher.

🍎 **TEACHER TIP:** Provide the number of syllables to blend: "Blend the 3 syllables, tor-na-do, into a whole word."

# Segmenting into Syllables

**LESSON FOCUS:** When we segment, we say a whole word and separate the word into the syllables we hear.

⇨ Segmenting Lesson 3: Segmenting Words into 3 Syllables

Teacher Directions: I will say the whole word. You will repeat the word and segment it into the syllables you hear.

Student Response: Student repeats the word aloud and segments the word into syllables.

| WHOLE WORD | CORRECT RESPONSE |
|---|---|
| hesitate | hez - ĭ - tāte |
| understand | ŭn - der - stănd |
| maximum | măx - ĭ - mŭm |

| WHOLE WORD | CORRECT RESPONSE |
|---|---|
| habitat | hăb - ĭ - tăt |
| important | ĭm - por - tĭnt |
| scenery | see - ner - ē |

✋ **SEGMENTING HAND MOTION:** Use hands in a chopping motion to represent the syllables; one chop for each syllable. Finger tapping for each syllable can also be used.

🍎 **TEACHER TIP:** Provide the number of syllables to segment: "Tell me the 3 syllables in the word hesitate."

# Blending Syllables

LESSON FOCUS: When we blend, we put parts of a word together to make a whole word.

⊛ Blending Lesson 4: Blending 3 Syllables into a Word

Teacher Directions: I will say the syllables, and you will blend the syllables into a word.

Student Response options:

1. Student repeats the syllables aloud and blends the syllables into a whole word.

2. Student hears the syllables and immediately blends the syllables into a whole word.

| SYLLABLES | CORRECT RESPONSE | SYLLABLES | CORRECT RESPONSE |
|---|---|---|---|
| hiss - ter - ē | history | vā - cā- tion | vacation |
| cum - plete - ly | completely | ĕl - ĕ - fent | elephant |
| jĭ - gan - tic | gigantic | mag - nĭ - fy | magnify |

✋ BLENDING HAND MOTION: Place palms together (or one hand can be used). The teacher chops hands from right to left, one chop for each syllable. Then slide hands right to left to say the whole word. Student mirrors the teacher.

🍎 TEACHER TIP: Provide the number of syllables to blend: "Blend the 3 syllables, how - ev - er, into a whole word."

LESSON FOCUS: When we segment, we say a whole word and separate the word into the syllables we hear.

# Segmenting into Syllables

⊛ Segmenting Lesson 4: Segmenting Words into 3 Syllables

Teacher Directions: I will say the whole word. You will repeat the word and segment it into the syllables you hear.

Student Response: Student repeats the word aloud and segments the word into syllables.

| WHOLE WORD | CORRECT RESPONSE | WHOLE WORD | CORRECT RESPONSE |
|---|---|---|---|
| resident | rez - ĭ -dent | particle | part - ĭ - cle |
| pioneer | pī - ŭ - neer | vocalist | vō - cul - ist |
| ownership | ōw - ner - ship | industry | in - dust - ree |

✋ SEGMENTING HAND MOTION: Use hands in a chopping motion to represent the syllables; one chop for each syllable. Finger tapping for each syllable can also be used.

🍎 TEACHER TIP: Provide the number of syllables to segment: "Tell me the 3 syllables in the word resident."

# Blending Syllables

LESSON FOCUS: When we blend, we put parts of a word together to make a whole word.

⊙ Blending Lesson 5: Blending 3 Syllables into a Word

Teacher Directions:  I will say the syllables, and you will blend the syllables into a word.

Student Response options:

1. Student repeats the syllables aloud and blends the syllables into a whole word.

2. Student hears the syllables and immediately blends the syllables into a whole word.

| SYLLABLES | CORRECT RESPONSE |
|-----------|------------------|
| how - ĕv - er | however |
| dŏm - ĭn - āte | dominate |
| har - vĭs - tĭd | harvested |

| SYLLABLES | CORRECT RESPONSE |
|-----------|------------------|
| nor - mal - ē | normally |
| căn - tŭ - lōpe | cantaloupe |
| ĕn - er - gē | energy |

🖐 BLENDING HAND MOTION: Place palms together (or one hand can be used).  The teacher chops hands from right to left, one chop for each syllable.  Then slide hands right to left to say the whole word.  Student mirrors the teacher.

🍎 TEACHER TIP: Provide the number of syllables to blend: "Blend the 3 syllables, how - ev - er, into a whole word."

# Segmenting into Syllables

LESSON FOCUS: When we segment, we say a whole word and separate the word into the syllables we hear.

⊙ Segmenting Lesson 5: Segmenting Words into 3 Syllables

Teacher Directions: I will say the whole word. You will repeat the word and segment it into the syllables you hear.

Student Response:  Student repeats the word aloud and segments the word into syllables.

| WHOLE WORD | CORRECT RESPONSE |
|-----------|------------------|
| dependent | de - pend - ent |
| trampoline | tram - pō - lean |
| celebrate | sell - ĭ - brate |

| WHOLE WORD | CORRECT RESPONSE |
|-----------|------------------|
| normally | nor - mull - ee |
| understand | un - der - stand |
| slippery | slip - er - ee |

🖐 SEGMENTING HAND MOTION: Use hands in a chopping motion to represent the syllables; one chop for each syllable.  Finger tapping for each syllable can also be used.

🍎 TEACHER TIP: Provide the number of syllables to segment.

# Blending Syllables

LESSON FOCUS: When we blend, we put parts of a word together to make a whole word.

⇨ Blending Lesson 6: Blending 4 Syllables into a Word

Teacher Directions:  I will say the syllables, and you will blend the syllables into a word.

Student Response options:

1.  Student repeats the syllables aloud and blends the syllables into a whole word.

2.  Student hears the syllables and immediately blends the syllables into a whole word.

| SYLLABLES | CORRECT RESPONSE |
|---|---|
| sci - in - tif - ic | scientific |
| ov - u - cŏ - dō | avocado |
| el - u - va - ter | elevator |

| SYLLABLES | CORRECT RESPONSE |
|---|---|
| vol - un - teer - ing | volunteering |
| gym - nā - zē - um | gymnasium |
| ē - mer - gen - see | emergency |

✋ BLENDING HAND MOTION: Place palms together (or one hand can be used).  The teacher chops hands from right to left, one chop for each syllable.  Then slide hands right to left to say the whole word.  Student mirrors the teacher.

🍎 TEACHER TIP: Provide the number of syllables to blend.

# Segmenting into Syllables

LESSON FOCUS: When we segment, we say a whole word and separate the word into the syllables we hear.

⇨ Segmenting Lesson 6: Segmenting Words into 4 Syllables

Teacher Directions: I will say the whole word. You will repeat the word and segment it into the syllables you hear.

Student Response:  Student repeats the word aloud and segments the word into syllables.

| WHOLE WORD | CORRECT RESPONSE |
|---|---|
| intervention | in - ter - ven - tion |
| harmonica | har - mon - i - cu |
| artificial | ar - ti - fi - cial |

| WHOLE WORD | CORRECT RESPONSE |
|---|---|
| prehistoric | pre - his - tor - ic |
| numerator | nu - mer - a - ter |
| motorcycle | mo - tor - cy - cle |

✋ SEGMENTING HAND MOTION: Use hands in a chopping motion to represent the syllables; one chop for each syllable.  Finger tapping for each syllable can also be used.

🍎 TEACHER TIP: Provide the number of syllables to segment: "Tell me the 4 syllables in the word intervention."

# Blending Syllables

LESSON FOCUS: When we blend, we put parts of a word together to make a whole word.

⇨ Blending Lesson 7: Blending 4 Syllables into a Word

Teacher Directions:  I will say the syllables, and you will blend the syllables into a word.

Student Response options:

1. Student repeats the syllables aloud and blends the syllables into a whole word.

2. Student hears the syllables and immediately blends the syllables into a whole word.

| SYLLABLES | CORRECT RESPONSE | SYLLABLES | CORRECT RESPONSE |
|---|---|---|---|
| cir - cum - stanc - es | circumstances | su - per - mar - ket | supermarket |
| com - pre - hen - sion | comprehension | con - ste - la - shun | constellation |
| in - de - pen - dent | independent | mis - cal - cu - late | miscalculate |

🖐 BLENDING HAND MOTION: Place palms together (or one hand can be used).  The teacher chops hands from right to left, one chop for each syllable.  Then slide hands right to left to say the whole word.  Student mirrors the teacher.

🍎 TEACHER TIP: Provide the number of syllables to blend: "Blend the 4 syllables, cir - cum - stance -es, into a whole word."

# Segmenting into Syllables

LESSON FOCUS: When we segment, we say a whole word and separate the word into the syllables we hear.

⇨ Segmenting Lesson 7: Segmenting Words into 4 Syllables

Teacher Directions: I will say the whole word. You will repeat the word and segment it into the syllables you hear.

Student Response:  Student repeats the word aloud and segments the word into syllables.

| WHOLE WORD | CORRECT RESPONSE | WHOLE WORD | CORRECT RESPONSE |
|---|---|---|---|
| calculator | cal - cu - la - ter | considerate | con - sid - er - it |
| graduation | grad - ū - ā - tion | territory | ter - ĭ - tor - ē |
| responsible | re - spon - si - ble | evaporate | ē - vap - or - ate |

🖐 SEGMENTING HAND MOTION: Use hands in a chopping motion to represent the syllables; one chop for each syllable.  Finger tapping for each syllable can also be used.

🍎 TEACHER TIP: Provide the number of syllables to segment: "Tell me the 4 syllables in the word calculator."

# Blending Syllables

LESSON FOCUS: When we blend, we put parts of a word together to make a whole word.

⇨ Blending Lesson 8: Blending Syllables into a Word

Teacher Directions: I will say the syllables, and you will blend the syllables into a word.

Student Response options:

1. Student repeats the syllables aloud and blends the syllables into a whole word.

2. Student hears the syllables and immediately blends the syllables into a whole word.

| SYLLABLES | CORRECT RESPONSE |
|---|---|
| trī - ang - le | triangle |
| ŭ - brē - vē - ate | abbreviate |
| crow - did | crowded |

| SYLLABLES | CORRECT RESPONSE |
|---|---|
| gē - ŏg - rŭ - fē | geography |
| ē - qual - ĭ - tē | equality |
| dif - ĭ - cult | difficult |

✋ BLENDING HAND MOTION: Place palms together (or one hand can be used). The teacher chops hands from right to left, one chop for each syllable. Then slide hands right to left to say the whole word. Student mirrors the teacher.

🍎 TEACHER TIP: Provide the number of syllables to blend: "Blend the 3 syllables: tri - ang - le into a whole word."

# Segmenting into Syllables

LESSON FOCUS: When we segment, we say a whole word and separate the word into the syllables we hear. In these lessons, we will segment words into 2, 3, or 4 syllables.

⇨ Segmenting Lesson 8: Segmenting Words into Syllables

Teacher Directions: I will say the whole word. You will repeat the word and segment it into the syllables you hear.

Student Response: Student repeats the word aloud and segments the word into syllables.

| WHOLE WORD | CORRECT RESPONSE |
|---|---|
| horizon | her - ī - zĭn |
| appreciate | ŭ - prē - she - ate |
| explanation | ex - plŭ - nā - tion |

| WHOLE WORD | CORRECT RESPONSE |
|---|---|
| legacy | leg - ŭ - sē |
| circle | sir - cle |
| demonstration | dem - un - strā - tion |

✋ SEGMENTING HAND MOTION: Use hands in a chopping motion to represent the syllables; one chop for each syllable. Finger tapping for each syllable can also be used.

🍎 TEACHER TIP: Provide the number of syllables to segment: "Tell me the 3 syllables in the word horizon."

# Blending Syllables

LESSON FOCUS: When we blend, we put parts of a word together to make a whole word.

⇨ Blending Lesson 9: Blending Syllables into a Word

Teacher Directions:  I will say the syllables, and you will blend the syllables into a word.

Student Response options:

1.  Student repeats the syllables aloud and blends the syllables into a whole word.

2.  Student hears the syllables and immediately blends the syllables into a whole word.

| SYLLABLES | CORRECT RESPONSE |
|---|---|
| max - ĭ - mum | maximum |
| un - der- stand | understand |
| el - ĕ - vate | elevate |

| SYLLABLES | CORRECT RESPONSE |
|---|---|
| whis - per - ing | whispering |
| rē - her - sal | rehearsal |
| judg - men - tal | judgmental |

🤚 BLENDING HAND MOTION: Place palms together (or one hand can be used).  The teacher chops hands from right to left, one chop for each syllable.  Then slide hands right to left to say the whole word.  Student mirrors the teacher.

🍎 TEACHER TIP: Provide the number of syllables to blend: "Blend the 3 syllables: max - i - mum into a whole word."

# Segmenting into Syllables

LESSON FOCUS: When we segment, we say a whole word and separate the word into the syllables we hear. In these lessons, we will segment words into 2, 3, or 4 syllables.

⇨ Segmenting Lesson 9: Segmenting Words into Syllables

Teacher Directions: I will say the whole word. You will repeat the word and segment it into the syllables you hear.

Student Response:  Student repeats the word aloud and segments the word into syllables.

| WHOLE WORD | CORRECT RESPONSE |
|---|---|
| vocal | vō - cal |
| ornament | or - nŭ - ment |
| extremely | ex - treme - ly |

| WHOLE WORD | CORRECT RESPONSE |
|---|---|
| positive | poz - ĭ - tiv |
| description | dē - scrip - tion |
| volunteer | vol - un - teer |

🤚 SEGMENTING HAND MOTION: Use hands in a chopping motion to represent the syllables; one chop for each syllable.  Finger tapping for each syllable can also be used.

🍎 TEACHER TIP: Provide the number of syllables to segment: "Tell me the 3 syllables in the word extremely."

# Blending Syllables

LESSON FOCUS: When we blend, we put parts of a word together to make a whole word.

⊙ Blending Lesson 10: Blending Syllables into a Word

Teacher Directions: I will say the syllables, and you will blend the syllables into a word.

Student Response options:

1. Student repeats the syllables aloud and blends the syllables into a whole word.

2. Student hears the syllables and immediately blends the syllables into a whole word.

| SYLLABLES | CORRECT RESPONSE | | SYLLABLES | CORRECT RESPONSE |
|---|---|---|---|---|
| vī - rus | virus | | en - cur - ŭ - jing | encouraging |
| cŭm - plain - ing | complaining | | in - ter - act | interact |
| a - gree - ment | agreement | | trans - por - tā - tion | transportation |

✋ BLENDING HAND MOTION: Place palms together (or one hand can be used). The teacher chops hands from right to left, one chop for each syllable. Then slide hands right to left to say the whole word. Student mirrors the teacher.

🍎 TEACHER TIP: Provide the number of syllables to blend: "Blend the 2 syllables: vi - rus into a whole word."

# Segmenting into Syllables

LESSON FOCUS: When we segment, we say a whole word and separate the word into the syllables we hear. In these lessons, we will segment words into 2, 3, or 4 syllables.

⊙ Segmenting Lesson 10: Segmenting Words into Syllables

Teacher Directions: I will say the whole word. You will repeat the word and segment it into the syllables you hear.

Student Response: Student repeats the word aloud and segments the word into syllables.

| WHOLE WORD | CORRECT RESPONSE | | WHOLE WORD | CORRECT RESPONSE |
|---|---|---|---|---|
| achievement | ŭ - chieve - ment | | instruction | in - struc - tion |
| explicit | ex - plĭ - sit | | unhappiness | un - happ - ē - ness |
| replacement | re - place - ment | | entertainment | en - ter - tain - ment |

✋ SEGMENTING HAND MOTION: Use hands in a chopping motion to represent the syllables; one chop for each syllable. Finger tapping for each syllable can also be used.

🍎 TEACHER TIP: Provide the number of syllables to segment: "Tell me the 3 syllables in the word achievement."

# Blending Syllables into Words

We have worked on many lessons with blending syllables. Today, you will show me what you have learned.

Teacher Administration Directions: I will say the syllables. You will blend them into a complete word. If you would like to repeat the syllables back to me first, you can.

Record incorrect responses in the Student Response column. If correct, mark with a check or +

Student Name: _____  Date: _____

|  | SYLLABLES | CORRECT RESPONSE | STUDENT RESPONSE |
|---|---|---|---|
| 1 | frac - tion | fraction | |
| 2 | tip - ĭ - cul | typical | |
| 3 | guv - ern | govern | |
| 4 | per - sis - tint | persistent | |
| 5 | found - da - tion | foundation | |
| 6 | will - ow | willow | |
| 7 | man - ū - fac - sure | manufacture | |
| 8 | in - ō - vā - tion | innovation | |
| 9 | mŭ - jor - ĭ - tē | majority | |
| 10 | ē - lim - ĭ - nate | eliminate | |
| | | TOTAL SCORE: | /10 |

SCORING GUIDE:

0-5 correct: Review Blending Syllables Lessons 1-10

6-8 correct: Review Blending Syllables Lessons 6-10

9-10 correct: Move on to Blending Phonemes in Lessons 11-25

# Segmenting Words into Syllables

We have worked on many lessons with segmenting words into syllables. Today, you are going to show me what you have learned.

Teacher Administration Directions: I will say a word. You will segment the word into syllables.

Record incorrect responses in the Student Response column. If correct, mark with a check or +

Student Name: _____     Date: _____

| | WHOLE WORD | CORRECT RESPONSE | STUDENT RESPONSE |
|---|---|---|---|
| 1 | respectful | re - spect - ful | |
| 2 | bicycle | bī - sik - cle | |
| 3 | feature | fē - ture | |
| 4 | curious | cure - ē - us | |
| 5 | disadvantage | dis - ad - van - tage | |
| 6 | agriculture | ag - rĭ - cul - ture | |
| 7 | dandelion | dan - dŭ - lī - in | |
| 8 | extract | ex - tract | |
| 9 | shivering | shiv - er - ing | |
| 10 | championship | cham - pea - un - ship | |
| | | TOTAL SCORE: | /10 |

## SCORING GUIDE:

0-5 correct: Review Segmenting Words into Syllables Lessons 1-10

6-8 correct: Review Segmenting Words into Syllables into a Word Lessons 6-10

9-10 correct: Move on to Segmenting Words into Phonemes in Lessons 11-25

# Anchor Lesson: Blending Phonemes into Words

LESSON FOCUS: When we blend, we put sounds of a word together to make a whole word. In these lessons, we will blend phonemes into a word.

## I DO:

I will say three phonemes or sounds and blend them together to make a whole word.

| m – ĭ - ss<br>miss | Watch me. When I blend the sounds /m/ - /ĭ/ - /s/. The word is miss.<br>Listen: /m/ - /ĭ/ - /s/ , miss. |
|---|---|
| p - ea-ch<br>peach | Watch me. When I blend the sounds /p/ - /ē/ - /ch/. The word is peach.<br>Listen: /p/ - /ē/ - /ch/, peach. |

## WE DO:

Let's try some words together. I will say three phonemes or sounds. We will repeat the three sounds and blend them together into a whole word.

| p - ar - t<br>part | T: Repeat after me: /p/ - /ar/ - /t/<br>T & S: /p/ - /ar/ - /t/<br>T: What's the word?<br>T & S: part |
|---|---|
| r - ai - n<br>rain | T: Repeat after me: /r/ - /ā/ - /n/<br>T & S: /r/ - /ā/ - /n/<br>T: What's the word?<br>T & S: rain |

## YOU DO:

I will say three phonemes or sounds. You will repeat the sounds and blend them into a whole word.

*Students can immediately blend the sounds into the word without repeating.*

| m - ee - t<br>meet | T: /m/ - /ē/ - /t/<br>S: /m/ - /ē/ - /t/ , meet |
|---|---|
| r - ī - d<br>ride | T: /r/ - /ī/ - /d/<br>S: /r/ - /ī/ - /d/ , ride |
| ch - oi - s<br>choice | T: /ch/ - /oi/ - /s/<br>S: /ch/ - /oi/ - /s/, choice |

*/m/ = say sound not letter name

---

**BLENDING HAND MOTION:**

Place palms together (or one hand can be used). The teacher chops hands from right to left, one chop for each sound. Then slide hands right to left to say the whole word. Student mirrors the teacher.

---

### TEACHER TIPS:

① Blending is parts to whole. The teacher says the sounds first, and then the sounds are blended into a whole word.

② Use a colored square (felt squares, magnetic tiles, counters, cubes, or chips) to provide a visual anchor for the sounds. Each square represents a sound. Teacher and/or students touch each cube, counter or tile when saying each sound aloud.

# Anchor Lesson: Segmenting Words into Phonemes

LESSON FOCUS: When we segment, we say a whole word and separate the word into all of the sounds we hear.

## I DO:

I will say a word and segment the word into all of the phonemes or sounds I hear.

| win | Watch me. The word is win. When I segment the word win into all of the sounds I hear, I hear 3 sounds: /w/ - /ĭ/ - /n/ |
|-----|-----|
| dug | Watch me. The word is dug. When I segment the word dug into all of the sounds I hear, I hear 3 sounds: /d/ - /ŭ/ - /g/ |

## WE DO:

Let's try some words together. I will say the word. You will repeat the word and together we will segment it into the sounds you hear.

| read | T: Say, read  T & S: read  T: Segment read into the sounds you hear.  T & S: /r/ - /ē/ - /d/ |
|------|-----|
| mop | T: Say, mop  T & S: mop  T: Segment mop into the sounds you hear.  T & S: /m/ - /ŏ/ - /p/ |

## YOU DO:

I will say a word. You will repeat the word and segment the word into the sounds you hear.

| nice | T: nice  S: nice, /n/ - /ī/ - /s/ |
|------|-----|
| bird | T: bird  S: bird, /b/ - /ir/ - /d/ |
| with | T: with  S: with, /w/ -/ĭ/ -/th/ |

---

**SEGMENTING HAND MOTION:**

Use hands in a chopping motion to represent the sounds or phonemes; one chop for each sound. Finger tapping for each sound can also be used.

---

## TEACHER TIPS:

1. Segmenting is whole to parts. The teacher says the whole word aloud, and the students segment the word into individual sounds.

2. Use a colored square (felt squares, magnetic tiles, counters, cubes, or chips) to provide a visual anchor for the sounds. Each square represents a sound. Teacher and/or students touch each cube, counter or tile when saying each sound aloud.

# Blending Phonemes

LESSON FOCUS: When we blend, we put sounds of a word together to make a whole word.

⮕ Blending Lesson 11: Blending 3 Phonemes into a Word

*Teacher Note: A phoneme is defined as the smallest unit of sound. Teachers may choose to use the word phoneme or sound when working with the lessons.*

Teacher Directions: I will say the sounds/phonemes, and you will blend the sounds/phonemes into a word.

Student Response options:

1. Student repeats the phonemes aloud and blends the phonemes into a whole word.

2. Student hears the phonemes and immediately blends the phonemes into a whole word.

| PHONEMES/SOUNDS | CORRECT RESPONSE | PHONEMES/SOUNDS | CORRECT RESPONSE |
|---|---|---|---|
| k - oi - n | coin | h - ē - p | heep |
| w - i - th | with | l - oo - z | lose |
| t - or - n | torn | sh - ar - p | sharp |

✋ BLENDING HAND MOTION: Place palms together (or one hand can be used). The teacher chops hands from right to left, one chop for each sound. Then slide hands right to left to say the whole word. Student mirrors the teacher.

🍎 TEACHER TIPS:

① "Can you blend these 3 or 4 sounds into a word?"

② Use the visual supports (felt squares, colored chips) to anchor the sounds.

# Segmenting into Phonemes

LESSON FOCUS: When we segment, we say a whole word and separate the word into all the sounds we hear.

⮕ Segmenting Lesson 11: Segmenting Words into 3 Phonemes

Teacher Directions: I will say the whole word and you will segment the word into the phonemes/sounds you hear.

Student Response: Student repeats the word aloud and segments the word into 3 phonemes/sounds.

| WHOLE WORD | CORRECT RESPONSE | WHOLE WORD | CORRECT RESPONSE |
|---|---|---|---|
| sail | s - ā - l | time | t - ī - m |
| those | th - ō - z | bird | b - ir - d |
| heart | h - ar - t | soon | s - oo - n |

✋ SEGMENTING HAND MOTION: Use hands in a chopping motion to represent the phonemes; one chop for each phoneme. Finger tapping for each phoneme can also be used.

🍎 TEACHER TIP: Include the number of sounds: "Tell me the 3 sounds you hear in the word sail."

# Blending Phonemes

LESSON FOCUS: When we blend, we put sounds of a word together to make a whole word.

⇨ Blending Lesson 12: Blending 3 Phonemes into a Word

Teacher Directions: I will say the sounds/phonemes, and you will blend the sounds/phonemes into a word.

Student Response options:

1. Student repeats the phonemes aloud and blends the phonemes into a whole word.

2. Student hears the phonemes and immediately blends the phonemes into a whole word.

| PHONEMES/SOUNDS | CORRECT RESPONSE | PHONEMES/SOUNDS | CORRECT RESPONSE |
| --- | --- | --- | --- |
| p - ou - t | pout | d - ī - s | dice |
| l - oo - k | look | w - er - k | work |
| b - ar - k | bark | p - ur - s | purse |

✋ BLENDING HAND MOTION: Place palms together (or one hand can be used). The teacher chops hands from right to left, one chop for each sound. Then slide hands right to left to say the whole word. Student mirrors the teacher.

🍎 TEACHER TIPS:

① "Can you blend these 3 sounds into a word?"

② Use the visual supports (felt squares, colored chips) to anchor the sounds.

# Segmenting into Phonemes

LESSON FOCUS: When we segment, we say a whole word and separate the word into all the sounds we hear.

⇨ Segmenting Lesson 12: Segmenting Words into 3 Phonemes

Teacher Directions: I will say the whole word and you will segment the word into the phonemes/sounds you hear.

Student Response: Student repeats the word aloud and segments the word into 3 phonemes/sounds.

| WHOLE WORD | CORRECT RESPONSE | WHOLE WORD | CORRECT RESPONSE |
| --- | --- | --- | --- |
| march | m - ar - ch | pool | p - oo - l |
| talk | t - aw - k | dove | d - ŭ - v |
| fork | f - or - k | verb | v - er - b |

✋ SEGMENTING HAND MOTION: Use hands in a chopping motion to represent the phonemes; one chop for each phoneme. Finger tapping for each phoneme can also be used.

🍎 TEACHER TIP: Include the number of sounds: "Tell me the 3 sounds you hear in the word sail."

# Blending Phonemes

LESSON FOCUS: When we blend, we put sounds of a word together to make a whole word.

⇨ Blending Lesson 13:  Blending 3 or 4 Phonemes into a Word

We are going to continue to blend and segment words, and now we will hear words that have three or four sounds.

Teacher Directions: I will say the sounds/phonemes, and you will blend the sounds/phonemes into a word.

Student Response options:

1.  Student repeats the phonemes aloud and blends the phonemes into a whole word.

2.  Student hears the phonemes and immediately blends the phonemes into a whole word.

| PHONEMES/SOUNDS | CORRECT RESPONSE | PHONEMES/SOUNDS | CORRECT RESPONSE |
|---|---|---|---|
| p - au - z | pause | t - oo - b | tube |
| sh - ou - t | shout | b - r - ĭ - j | bridge |
| s - aw - f - t | soft | t - w - ĭ - n | twin |

🖐 BLENDING HAND MOTION: Place palms together (or one hand can be used).  The teacher chops hands from right to left, one chop for each sound.  Then slide hands right to left to say the whole word.  Student mirrors the teacher.

🍎 TEACHER TIPS:
① "Can you blend these 3 or 4 sounds into a word?"
② Use the visual supports (felt squares, colored chips) to anchor the sounds.

# Segmenting into Phonemes

LESSON FOCUS: When we segment, we say a whole word and separate the word into all the sounds we hear.

⇨ Segmenting Lesson 13: Segmenting Words into 3 or 4 Phonemes

Teacher Directions:  I will say the whole word and you will segment the word into the phonemes/sounds you hear.

Student Response:  Student repeats the word aloud and segments the word into 3 or 4 phonemes/sounds.

| WHOLE WORD | CORRECT RESPONSE | WHOLE WORD | CORRECT RESPONSE |
|---|---|---|---|
| clash | c - l - ă - sh | swim | s - w - ĭ - m |
| slight | s - l - ī - t | port | p - or - t |
| noise | n - oi - z | smart | s - m - ar - t |

🖐 SEGMENTING HAND MOTION: Use hands in a chopping motion to represent the phonemes; one chop for each phoneme.  Finger tapping for each phoneme can also be used.

🍎 TEACHER TIP:  Include the number of sounds: "Tell me the 4 sounds you hear in the word clash."

# Blending Phonemes

LESSON FOCUS: When we blend, we put sounds of a word together to make a whole word.

⇨ Blending Lesson 14: Blending 4 Phonemes into a Word

Teacher Directions: I will say the sounds/phonemes, and you will blend the sounds/phonemes into a word.

Student Response options:

1.  Student repeats the phonemes aloud and blends the phonemes into a whole word.

2.  Student hears the phonemes and immediately blends the phonemes into a whole word.

| PHONEMES/SOUNDS | CORRECT RESPONSE | PHONEMES/SOUNDS | CORRECT RESPONSE |
| --- | --- | --- | --- |
| s - m - ŭ - j | smudge | f - l - aw - s | floss |
| k - l - ŭ - ch | clutch | s - n - oo - p | snoop |
| ch - ă - m - p | champ | f - ă - c - t | fact |

BLENDING HAND MOTION: Place palms together (or one hand can be used). The teacher chops hands from right to left, one chop for each sound. Then slide hands right to left to say the whole word. Student mirrors the teacher.

TEACHER TIPS:

①  "Can you blend these 3 or 4 sounds into a word?"

②  Use the visual supports (felt squares, colored chips) to anchor the sounds.

# Segmenting into Phonemes

LESSON FOCUS: When we segment, we say a whole word and separate the word into all the sounds we hear.

⇨ Segmenting Lesson 14: Segmenting Words into 4 Phonemes

Teacher Directions: I will say the whole word and you will segment the word into the phonemes/sounds you hear.

Student Response: Student repeats the word aloud and segments the word into 4 phonemes/sounds.

| WHOLE WORD | CORRECT RESPONSE | WHOLE WORD | CORRECT RESPONSE |
| --- | --- | --- | --- |
| clown | k - l - ow - n | storm | s - t - or - m |
| left | l - ě - f - t | flash | f - l - ă - sh |
| twice | t - w - ī - s | spout | s - p - ou - t |

SEGMENTING HAND MOTION: Use hands in a chopping motion to represent the phonemes; one chop for each phoneme. Finger tapping for each phoneme can also be used.

TEACHER TIP: Include the number of sounds: "Tell me the 4 sounds you hear in the word clown."

# Blending Phonemes

LESSON FOCUS: When we blend, we put sounds of a word together to make a whole word.

⊕ Blending Lesson 15: Blending 4 Phonemes into a Word

Teacher Directions: I will say the sounds/phonemes, and you will blend the sounds/phonemes into a word.

Student Response options:

1. Student repeats the phonemes aloud and blends the phonemes into a whole word.

2. Student hears the phonemes and immediately blends the phonemes into a whole word.

| PHONEMES/SOUNDS | CORRECT RESPONSE | PHONEMES/SOUNDS | CORRECT RESPONSE |
|---|---|---|---|
| w - ĕ - s - t | west | s - t - ŏ - p | stop |
| f - l - ī - t | flight | c - l - ā - m | claim |
| g - r - ă - b | grab | l - ă - m - p | lamp |

✋ BLENDING HAND MOTION: Place palms together (or one hand can be used). The teacher chops hands from right to left, one chop for each sound. Then slide hands right to left to say the whole word. Student mirrors the teacher.

🍎 TEACHER TIPS:
① "Can you blend these 3 or 4 sounds into a word?"
② Use the visual supports (felt squares, colored chips) to anchor the sounds.

# Segmenting into Phonemes

LESSON FOCUS: When we segment, we say a whole word and separate the word into all the sounds we hear.

⊕ Segmenting Lesson 15: Segmenting Words into 4 Phonemes

Teacher Directions: I will say the whole word and you will segment the word into the phonemes/sounds you hear.

Student Response: Student repeats the word aloud and segments the word into 4 phonemes/sounds.

| WHOLE WORD | CORRECT RESPONSE | WHOLE WORD | CORRECT RESPONSE |
|---|---|---|---|
| stuck | s - t - ŭ - k | last | l - ă - s - t |
| grass | g - r - ă - s | speech | s - p - ē - ch |
| clock | k - l - ŏ - k | praise | p - r - ā - z |

✋ SEGMENTING HAND MOTION: Use hands in a chopping motion to represent the phonemes; one chop for each phoneme. Finger tapping for each phoneme can also be used.

🍎 TEACHER TIP: Include the number of sounds: "Tell me the 4 sounds you hear in the word stuck."

# Blending Phonemes

LESSON FOCUS: When we blend, we put sounds of a word together to make a whole word.

⊜ Blending Lesson 16: Blending 4 Phonemes into a Word

Teacher Directions: I will say the sounds/phonemes, and you will blend the sounds/phonemes into a word.

Student Response options:

1. Student repeats the phonemes aloud and blends the phonemes into a whole word.

2. Student hears the phonemes and immediately blends the phonemes into a whole word.

| PHONEMES/SOUNDS | CORRECT RESPONSE | PHONEMES/SOUNDS | CORRECT RESPONSE |
|---|---|---|---|
| g - l - ŭ - v | glove | l - ĕ - f - t | left |
| s - m - oo - th | smooth | p - oi - n - t | point |
| f - r - ē - z | freeze | s - p - or - t | sport |

✋ BLENDING HAND MOTION: Place palms together (or one hand can be used). The teacher chops hands from right to left, one chop for each sound. Then slide hands right to left to say the whole word. Student mirrors the teacher.

🍎 TEACHER TIPS:

① "Can you blend these 3 or 4 sounds into a word?"

② Use the visual supports (felt squares, colored chips) to anchor the sounds.

# Segmenting into Phonemes

LESSON FOCUS: When we segment, we say a whole word and separate the word into all the sounds we hear.

⊜ Segmenting Lesson 16: Segmenting Words into 4 Phonemes

Teacher Directions: I will say the whole word and you will segment the word into the phonemes/sounds you hear.

Student Response: Student repeats the word aloud and segments the word into 4 phonemes/sounds.

| WHOLE WORD | CORRECT RESPONSE | WHOLE WORD | CORRECT RESPONSE |
|---|---|---|---|
| spoil | s - p - oi - l | nest | n - ĕ - s - t |
| spout | s - p - ou - t | jump | j - ŭ - m - p |
| cloud | k - l - ou - d | steam | s - t - ē - m |

✋ SEGMENTING HAND MOTION: Use hands in a chopping motion to represent the phonemes; one chop for each phoneme. Finger tapping for each phoneme can also be used.

🍎 TEACHER TIP: Include the number of sounds: "Tell me the 4 sounds you hear in the word stuck."

# Blending Phonemes

LESSON FOCUS: When we blend, we put sounds of a word together to make a whole word.

⇨ Blending Lesson 17: Blending 4 or 5 Phonemes into a Word

Teacher Directions: I will say the sounds/phonemes, and you will blend the sounds/phonemes into a word.

Student Response options:

1. Student repeats the phonemes aloud and blends the phonemes into a whole word.

2. Student hears the phonemes and immediately blends the phonemes into a whole word.

| PHONEMES/SOUNDS | CORRECT RESPONSE | PHONEMES/SOUNDS | CORRECT RESPONSE |
|---|---|---|---|
| s - c - ou - t | scout | r - ĭ - s - k | risk |
| b - l - ŏ - n - d | blonde | k - aw - s - t | cost |
| g - l - ă - n - s | glance | k - r - ĭ - s - p | crisp |

🖐 BLENDING HAND MOTION: Place palms together (or one hand can be used). The teacher chops hands from right to left, one chop for each sound. Then slide hands right to left to say the whole word. Student mirrors the teacher.

🍎 TEACHER TIPS:

① "Can you blend these 4 or 5 sounds into a word?"

② Use the visual supports (felt squares, colored chips) to anchor the sounds.

# Segmenting into Phonemes

LESSON FOCUS: When we segment, we say a whole word and separate the word into all the sounds we hear.

⇨ Segmenting Lesson 17: Segmenting Words into 4 and 5 Phonemes

Teacher Directions: I will say the whole word and you will segment the word into all of the phonemes/sounds you hear.

Student Response: Student repeats the word aloud and segments the word into 4 or 5 phonemes/sounds.

| WHOLE WORD | CORRECT RESPONSE | WHOLE WORD | CORRECT RESPONSE |
|---|---|---|---|
| scram | s - k - r - ă - m | crust | k - r - ŭ - s - t |
| gasp | g - ă - s - p | tweed | t - w - ē - d |
| switch | s - w - ĭ - ch | thrash | th - r - ă - sh |

🖐 SEGMENTING HAND MOTION: Use hands in a chopping motion to represent the phonemes; one chop for each phoneme. Finger tapping for each phoneme can also be used.

🍎 TEACHER TIP: Include the number of sounds: "Tell me the 5 sounds you hear in the word scram."

# Blending Phonemes

LESSON FOCUS: When we blend, we put sounds of a word together to make a whole word.

⇨ Blending Lesson 18: Blending 4 or 5 Phonemes into a Word

Teacher Directions: I will say the sounds/phonemes, and you will blend the sounds/phonemes into a word.

Student Response options:

1. Student repeats the phonemes aloud and blends the phonemes into a whole word.

2. Student hears the phonemes and immediately blends the phonemes into a whole word.

| PHONEMES/SOUNDS | CORRECT RESPONSE | | PHONEMES/SOUNDS | CORRECT RESPONSE |
|---|---|---|---|---|
| b - ĕ - s - t | best | | g - l - ē - m | gleam |
| s - t - ĭ - tch | stitch | | p - r - ō - b | probe |
| s - l - ĕ - p - t | slept | | f - l - ŭ - d | flood |

✋ BLENDING HAND MOTION: Place palms together (or one hand can be used). The teacher chops hands from right to left, one chop for each sound. Then slide hands right to left to say the whole word. Student mirrors the teacher.

🍎 TEACHER TIPS:

① "Can you blend these 4 or 5 sounds into a word?"

② Use the visual supports (felt squares, colored chips) to anchor the sounds.

# Segmenting into Phonemes

LESSON FOCUS: When we segment, we say a whole word and separate the word into all the sounds we hear.

⇨ Segmenting Lesson 18: Segmenting Words into 4 and 5 Phonemes

Teacher Directions: I will say the whole word and you will segment the word into all of the phonemes/sounds you hear.

Student Response: Student repeats the word aloud and segments the word into 4 or 5 phonemes/sounds.

| WHOLE WORD | CORRECT RESPONSE | | WHOLE WORD | CORRECT RESPONSE |
|---|---|---|---|---|
| proud | p - r - ou - d | | breathe | b - r - ē - th* |
| twice | t - w - ī - s | | sketch | s - k - ĕ - tch |
| claim | c - l - ā - m | | sponge | s - p - ŭ - n - j |

\* voiced /th/

✋ SEGMENTING HAND MOTION: Use hands in a chopping motion to represent the phonemes; one chop for each phoneme. Finger tapping for each phoneme can also be used.

🍎 TEACHER TIP: Include the number of sounds: "Tell me the 4 sounds you hear in the word proud."

# Blending Phonemes

LESSON FOCUS: When we blend, we put sounds of a word together to make a whole word.

⊕ Blending Lesson 19: Blending 5 Phonemes into a Word

Teacher Directions: I will say the sounds/phonemes, and you will blend the sounds/phonemes into a word.

Student Response options:

1. Student repeats the phonemes aloud and blends the phonemes into a whole word.

2. Student hears the phonemes and immediately blends the phonemes into a whole word.

| PHONEMES/SOUNDS | CORRECT RESPONSE |
|---|---|
| s - w - ĭ - f - t | swift |
| k - r - ŭ - n - ch | crunch |
| s - p - r - ou - t | sprout |

| PHONEMES/SOUNDS | CORRECT RESPONSE |
|---|---|
| t - w - ĭ - s -t | twist |
| s - t - ŏ - m - p | stomp |
| s - p - l - ă - sh | splash |

✋ BLENDING HAND MOTION: Place palms together (or one hand can be used). The teacher chops hands from right to left, one chop for each sound. Then slide hands right to left to say the whole word. Student mirrors the teacher.

🍎 TEACHER TIPS:

① "Can you blend these 5 sounds into a word?"

② Use the visual supports (felt squares, colored chips) to anchor the sounds.

# Segmenting into Phonemes

LESSON FOCUS: When we segment, we say a whole word and separate the word into all the sounds we hear.

⊕ Segmenting Lesson 19: Segmenting Words into 5 Phonemes

Teacher Directions: I will say the whole word and you will segment the word into all of the phonemes/sounds you hear.

Student Response: Student repeats the word aloud and segments the word into 5 phonemes/sounds.

| WHOLE WORD | CORRECT RESPONSE |
|---|---|
| spruce | s - p - r - oo - s |
| thrift | th - r - ĭ - f - t |
| split | s - p - l - ĭ - t |

| WHOLE WORD | CORRECT RESPONSE |
|---|---|
| spend | s - p - ĕ - n - d |
| plump | p - l - ŭ - m - p |
| scrape | s - k - r - ā - p |

✋ SEGMENTING HAND MOTION: Use hands in a chopping motion to represent the phonemes; one chop for each phoneme. Finger tapping for each phoneme can also be used.

🍎 TEACHER TIP: Include the number of sounds: "Tell me the 5 sounds you hear in the word scram."

# Blending Phonemes

LESSON FOCUS: When we blend, we put sounds of a word together to make a whole word.

⊕ Blending Lesson 20: Blending 5 Phonemes into a Word

Teacher Directions: I will say the sounds/phonemes, and you will blend the sounds/phonemes into a word.

Student Response options:

1.  Student repeats the phonemes aloud and blends the phonemes into a whole word.

2.  Student hears the phonemes and immediately blends the phonemes into a whole word.

| PHONEMES/SOUNDS | CORRECT RESPONSE |
| --- | --- |
| p - l - ŭ - m - p | plump |
| s - p - r - ā - n | sprain |
| g - r - ou - n - d | ground |

| PHONEMES/SOUNDS | CORRECT RESPONSE |
| --- | --- |
| b - r - ă - n - ch | branch |
| g - r - ă - s - p | grasp |
| s - c - ō - l - d | scold |

✋ BLENDING HAND MOTION: Place palms together (or one hand can be used). The teacher chops hands from right to left, one chop for each sound. Then slide hands right to left to say the whole word. Student mirrors the teacher.

🍎 TEACHER TIPS:

①  "Can you blend these 5 sounds into a word?"

②  Use the visual supports (felt squares, colored chips) to anchor the sounds.

# Segmenting into Phonemes

LESSON FOCUS: When we segment, we say a whole word and separate the word into all the sounds we hear.

⊕ Segmenting Lesson 20: Segmenting Words into 5 Phonemes

Teacher Directions: I will say the whole word and you will segment the word into all of the phonemes/sounds you hear.

Student Response: Student repeats the word aloud and segments the word into 5 phonemes/sounds.

| WHOLE WORD | CORRECT RESPONSE |
| --- | --- |
| crust | c - r - ŭ - s - t |
| friend | f - r - ě - n - d |
| craft | c - r - ă - f - t |

| WHOLE WORD | CORRECT RESPONSE |
| --- | --- |
| blonde | b - l - ŏ - n - d |
| clomp | k - l - ŏ - m - p |
| clasp | c - l - ă - s - p |

✋ SEGMENTING HAND MOTION: Use hands in a chopping motion to represent the phonemes; one chop for each phoneme. Finger tapping for each phoneme can also be used.

🍎 TEACHER TIP: Include the number of sounds: "Tell me the 5 sounds you hear in the word crust."

# Blending Phonemes

LESSON FOCUS: When we blend, we put sounds of a word together to make a whole word.

⊕ Blending Lesson 21: Blending Phonemes into Words

Teacher Directions: I will say the sounds/phonemes, and you will blend the sounds/phonemes into a word.

Student Response options:

1. Student repeats the phonemes aloud and blends the phonemes into a whole word.

2. Student hears the phonemes and immediately blends the phonemes into a whole word.

| PHONEMES/SOUNDS | CORRECT RESPONSE | PHONEMES/SOUNDS | CORRECT RESPONSE |
|---|---|---|---|
| p - ou - ch | pouch | s - t - oo - d | stood |
| m - oo - s | moose | t - w - ē - t | tweet |
| c - r - ow - n | crown | t - au - t | taught |

✋ BLENDING HAND MOTION: Place palms together (or one hand can be used). The teacher chops hands from right to left, one chop for each sound. Then slide hands right to left to say the whole word. Student mirrors the teacher.

🍎 TEACHER TIPS:

① "Can you blend these 3 or 4 sounds into a word?"

② Use the visual supports (felt squares, colored chips) to anchor the sounds.

# Segmenting into Phonemes

LESSON FOCUS: When we segment, we say a whole word and separate the word into all the sounds we hear.

⊕ Segmenting Lesson 21: Segmenting Words into Phonemes

Teacher Directions: I will say the whole word and you will segment the word into all of the phonemes/sounds you hear.

Student Response: Student repeats the word aloud and segments the word into phonemes/sounds.

| WHOLE WORD | CORRECT RESPONSE | WHOLE WORD | CORRECT RESPONSE |
|---|---|---|---|
| house | h - ou - s | grace | g - r - ā - s |
| should | sh - oo - d | smart | s - m - ar - t |
| found | f - ou - n - d | clause | c - l - au - z |

✋ SEGMENTING HAND MOTION: Use hands in a chopping motion to represent the phonemes; one chop for each phoneme. Finger tapping for each phoneme can also be used.

🍎 TEACHER TIP: Include the number of sounds: "Tell me the 5 sounds you hear in the word crust."

# Blending Phonemes

LESSON FOCUS: When we blend, we put sounds of a word together to make a whole word.

⊕ Blending Lesson 22: Blending Phonemes into Words

Teacher Directions: I will say the sounds/phonemes, and you will blend the sounds/phonemes into a word.

Student Response options:

1. Student repeats the phonemes aloud and blends the phonemes into a whole word.

2. Student hears the phonemes and immediately blends the phonemes into a whole word.

| PHONEMES/SOUNDS | CORRECT RESPONSE | PHONEMES/SOUNDS | CORRECT RESPONSE |
|---|---|---|---|
| p - au - z | pause | f - r - ĭ - n - j | fringe |
| b - ou - n - s | bounce | c - l - ŭ - b | club |
| s - p - r - ĭ - n - t | sprint | p - or - ch | porch |

✋ BLENDING HAND MOTION: Place palms together (or one hand can be used). The teacher chops hands from right to left, one chop for each sound. Then slide hands right to left to say the whole word. Student mirrors the teacher.

🍎 TEACHER TIPS:

① "Can you blend these 3, 4, 5, or 6 sounds into a word?"

② Use the visual supports (felt squares, colored chips) to anchor the sounds.

# Segmenting into Phonemes

LESSON FOCUS: When we segment, we say a whole word and separate the word into all the sounds we hear.

⊕ Segmenting Lesson 22: Segmenting Words into Phonemes

Teacher Directions: I will say the whole word and you will segment the word into all of the phonemes/sounds you hear.

Student Response: Student repeats the word aloud and segments the word into phonemes/sounds.

| WHOLE WORD | CORRECT RESPONSE | WHOLE WORD | CORRECT RESPONSE |
|---|---|---|---|
| grump | g - r - ŭ - m - p | guard | g - ar - d |
| south | s - ou - th | throat | th - r - ō - t |
| grouch | g - r - ou - ch | chest | ch - ĕ - s - t |

✋ SEGMENTING HAND MOTION: Use hands in a chopping motion to represent the phonemes; one chop for each phoneme. Finger tapping for each phoneme can also be used.

🍎 TEACHER TIP: Include the number of sounds: "Tell me the 5 sounds you hear in the word crust."

# Blending Phonemes

LESSON FOCUS: When we blend, we put sounds of a word together to make a whole word.

⊕ Blending Lesson 23: Blending Phonemes into Words

Teacher Directions: I will say the sounds/phonemes, and you will blend the sounds/phonemes into a word.

Student Response options:

1.  Student repeats the phonemes aloud and blends the phonemes into a whole word.

2.  Student hears the phonemes and immediately blends the phonemes into a whole word.

| PHONEMES/SOUNDS | CORRECT RESPONSE |
|---|---|
| h - aw - k - s | hawks |
| r - ea - ch | reach |
| s - w - ĕ - p - t | swept |

| PHONEMES/SOUNDS | CORRECT RESPONSE |
|---|---|
| th - ir - s - t | thirst |
| wh - ĭ - s - k | whisk |
| ch - oo - z | choose |

✋ BLENDING HAND MOTION: Place palms together (or one hand can be used). The teacher chops hands from right to left, one chop for each sound. Then slide hands right to left to say the whole word. Student mirrors the teacher.

🍎 TEACHER TIPS:

① "Can you blend these 3, 4, 5, or 6 sounds into a word?"

② Use the visual supports (felt squares, colored chips) to anchor the sounds.

# Segmenting into Phonemes

LESSON FOCUS: When we segment, we say a whole word and separate the word into all the sounds we hear.

⊕ Segmenting Lesson 23: Segmenting Words into Phonemes

Teacher Directions: I will say the whole word and you will segment the word into all of the phonemes/sounds you hear.

Student Response: Student repeats the word aloud and segments the word into phonemes/sounds.

| WHOLE WORD | CORRECT RESPONSE |
|---|---|
| brook | b - r - oo - k |
| clench | c - l - ĕ - n - ch |
| switch | s - w - ĭ - tch |

| WHOLE WORD | CORRECT RESPONSE |
|---|---|
| crest | c - r - ĕ - s - t |
| starve | s - t - ar - v |
| north | n - or - th |

✋ SEGMENTING HAND MOTION: Use hands in a chopping motion to represent the phonemes; one chop for each phoneme. Finger tapping for each phoneme can also be used.

🍎 TEACHER TIP: Include the number of sounds: "Tell me the 5 sounds you hear in the word crest."

# Blending Phonemes

LESSON FOCUS: When we blend, we put sounds of a word together to make a whole word.

⊕ Blending Lesson 24: Blending Phonemes into Words

Teacher Directions: I will say the sounds/phonemes, and you will blend the sounds/phonemes into a word.

Student Response options:

1. Student repeats the phonemes aloud and blends the phonemes into a whole word.

2. Student hears the phonemes and immediately blends the phonemes into a whole word.

| PHONEMES/SOUNDS | CORRECT RESPONSE | PHONEMES/SOUNDS | CORRECT RESPONSE |
|---|---|---|---|
| ch - oi - s | choice | g - l - ō - b | globe |
| s - l - ā - t | slate | s - t - or - k | stork |
| b - r - ĭ - j | bridge | b - l - ŭ - f | bluff |

✋ BLENDING HAND MOTION: Place palms together (or one hand can be used). The teacher chops hands from right to left, one chop for each sound. Then slide hands right to left to say the whole word. Student mirrors the teacher.

🍎 TEACHER TIPS:

① "Can you blend these 3 or 4 sounds into a word?"

② Use the visual supports (felt squares, colored chips) to anchor the sounds.

# Segmenting into Phonemes

LESSON FOCUS: When we segment, we say a whole word and separate the word into all the sounds we hear.

⊕ Segmenting Lesson 24: Segmenting Words into Phonemes

Teacher Directions: I will say the whole word and you will segment the word into all of the phonemes/sounds you hear.

Student Response: Student repeats the word aloud and segments the word into phonemes/sounds.

| WHOLE WORD | CORRECT RESPONSE | WHOLE WORD | CORRECT RESPONSE |
|---|---|---|---|
| shift | sh - ĭ - f - t | swamp | s - w - ŏ - m - p |
| round | r - ou - n - d | knelt | n - ĕ - l - t |
| scorch | s - c - or - ch | spread | s - p - r - ĕ - d |

✋ SEGMENTING HAND MOTION: Use hands in a chopping motion to represent the phonemes; one chop for each phoneme. Finger tapping for each phoneme can also be used.

🍎 TEACHER TIP: Include the number of sounds: "Tell me the 5 sounds you hear in the word crust."

# Blending Phonemes

LESSON FOCUS: When we blend, we put sounds of a word together to make a whole word.

⇨ Blending Lesson 25: Blending Phonemes into Words

Teacher Directions: I will say the sounds/phonemes, and you will blend the sounds/phonemes into a word.

Student Response options:

1.  Student repeats the phonemes aloud and blends the phonemes into a whole word.

2.  Student hears the phonemes and immediately blends the phonemes into a whole word.

| PHONEMES/SOUNDS | CORRECT RESPONSE | PHONEMES/SOUNDS | CORRECT RESPONSE |
|---|---|---|---|
| f - r - aw - s - t | frost | m - ĕ - n - t | meant |
| s - l - ŭ - m - p | slump | b - l - oo - m | bloom |
| b - r - oi - l | broil | c - ou - n - t | count |

✋ BLENDING HAND MOTION: Place palms together (or one hand can be used). The teacher chops hands from right to left, one chop for each sound. Then slide hands right to left to say the whole word. Student mirrors the teacher.

🍎 TEACHER TIPS:

① "Can you blend these 3, 4, 5, or 6 sounds into a word?"

② Use the visual supports (felt squares, colored chips) to anchor the sounds.

# Segmenting into Phonemes

LESSON FOCUS: When we segment, we say a whole word and separate the word into all the sounds we hear.

⇨ Segmenting Lesson 25: Segmenting Words into Phonemes

Teacher Directions: I will say the whole word and you will segment the word into all of the phonemes/sounds you hear.

Student Response: Student repeats the word aloud and segments the word into phonemes/sounds.

| WHOLE WORD | CORRECT RESPONSE | WHOLE WORD | CORRECT RESPONSE |
|---|---|---|---|
| knock | n - ŏ - ck | plush | p - l - ŭ - sh |
| ground | g - r - ou - n - d | blast | b - l - ă - s - t |
| fluke | f - l - oo - k | scream | s - c - r - ē - m |

✋ SEGMENTING HAND MOTION: Use hands in a chopping motion to represent the phonemes; one chop for each phoneme. Finger tapping for each phoneme can also be used.

🍎 TEACHER TIP: Include the number of sounds: "Tell me the 5 sounds you hear in the word crust."

# Blending Phonemes into Words

**BLENDING ASSESSMENT:** We have worked on many lessons with blending sounds into words. Today, you are going to show me what you have learned.

Teacher Administration Directions: I will say the sounds/phonemes. You will blend them into a complete word. If you would like to repeat the sounds back to me first, you can.

Record incorrect responses in the Student Response column. If correct, mark with a check or +

Student Name: _____ Date: _____

| | PHONEMES | CORRECT RESPONSE | STUDENT RESPONSE |
|---|---|---|---|
| 1 | f - ĭ - s - t | fist | |
| 2 | s - l - ē - v | sleeve | |
| 3 | s - p - l - ĭ - t | split | |
| 4 | s - t - ō - v | stove | |
| 5 | s - w - ĭ - sh | swish | |
| 6 | c - r - ow - d | crowd | |
| 7 | sh - r - ĕ - d | shred | |
| 8 | h - oi - s - t | hoist | |
| 9 | c - r - e - p - t | crept | |
| 10 | s - aw - f - t | soft | |
| | | TOTAL SCORE: | /10 |

**SCORING GUIDE:**

0-5 correct: Review Blending Phonemes Lessons 11-25

6-8 correct: Review Blending Phonemes Lessons 16-25

9-10 correct: Blending instruction is complete.

# Segmenting Words into Phonemes

**SEGMENTING ASSESSMENT:** We have worked on many lessons with segmenting a word into individual sounds/phonemes. Today, you are going to show me what you have learned.

Teacher Administration Directions: I will a say a whole word. You will repeat the word and segment the word into sounds/phonemes.

Record incorrect responses in the Student Response column. If correct, mark with a check or +

Student Name: _____     Date: _____

|  | WHOLE WORD | CORRECT RESPONSE | STUDENT RESPONSE |
|---|---|---|---|
| 1 | hoop | h - oo - p | |
| 2 | greed | g - r - ē - d | |
| 3 | foil | f - oi - l | |
| 4 | blast | b - l - ă - s - t | |
| 5 | spark | s - p - ar - k | |
| 6 | least | l - ē - s - t | |
| 7 | starch | s - t - ar - ch | |
| 8 | crisp | c - r - ĭ - s - p | |
| 9 | swerve | s - w - er - v | |
| 10 | thorn | th - or - n | |
| | | TOTAL SCORE: | /10 |

**SCORING GUIDE:**

0-5 correct: Review Segmenting into Phonemes Lessons 11-25

6-8 correct: Review Segmenting into Phonemes Lessons 16-25

9-10 correct: Segmenting instruction is complete.

# PART 3

# Phoneme Manipulation

# Defining Phoneme Manipulation

1. Phoneme Manipulation:

   We can manipulate phonemes or sounds by adding, deleting, or substituting a sound or phoneme in a word.

2. Adding Phonemes:

   We can add a phoneme/sound to a word or word part to make a new word. We will add initial phonemes, final phonemes, and phonemes to create a blend.

3. Deleting Phonemes:

   When we delete a phoneme/sound from a word, a new word or word part is left. We will delete initial phonemes, final phonemes, and a phoneme from a consonant blend.

4. Substituting Phonemes:

   When we substitute a phoneme/sound, we change a phoneme to make a new word. We will substitute phonemes in various places throughout a word to make a new word. This can be any sound in a word.

---

**TEACHER'S NOTE:**

Adding and substituting the initial sound in a word is required for rhyme production. If you are working with students who struggle to generate a rhyming word, you can share how adding an initial phoneme to a rime, creates a word that rhymes.

Example: When I add /g/ to /ot/ the word is got. /ot/ and got rhyme.

Students can also generate a word that rhymes by substituting the initial phoneme.

Example: said; change /s/ to /h/ and the word is head. Said and head are 2 words that rhyme because they have the same middle and final sounds (rime).

---

# Anchor Lesson: Adding Initial Phonemes

LESSON FOCUS: When we say a word or a word part, we can add a sound at the beginning to make a new word. In these lessons, we will make new words by adding a sound at the beginning of a word or word part.

### I DO:

I will show you how we can add a sound to the beginning of a word or word part to make a new word.

| nod | T: Watch me. When I say /-od/ and add /n/ at the beginning, the word is /n/-/od/, nod. |
| | I can also say that word quickly, without saying the parts. Watch me: |
| | /od/; add /n/ at the beginning and the word is nod. |
| game | T: When I say /-aim/ and add /g/ at the beginning, the word is /g/ - /aim/, game. |

### WE DO:

Let's try some words together. I will say a word. You will repeat the word. We will add a sound at the beginning and say the new word.

| cup | T: Say, up |
| | T & S: up |
| | T: Add /k/ at the beginning and the word is? |
| | T & S: cup |
| mall | T: Say, all |
| | T & S: all |
| | T: Add /m/ at the beginning and word is? |
| | T & S: mall |

### YOU DO:

Now it is your turn. I will say a word. You will repeat the word. I will tell you a sound to add at the beginning and you will tell me the new word.

| SAY: | ADD /*/ AT THE BEGINNING | THE WORD IS: |
|------|--------------------------|--------------|
| ace | /p/ | pace |
| and | /h/ | hand |
| oak | /s/ | soak |

✋ **ADDING HAND MOTION:**
Teacher holds left palm out to show the word/word part. Add the first sound with right hand and lightly clap hands together for the whole word.

🍎
**TEACHER TIPS:**

①  If students are struggling to create new word, you can scaffold support by saying the onset and rime, and then blend the two together. Example: /n/-/od/, nod

②  /*/ Say sound, not letter name

# Anchor Lesson: Deleting Initial Phonemes

LESSON FOCUS: When we hear a whole word, we can delete or take away a sound and say what is left. Sometimes taking away a sound makes a new word, and other times, it is just a word part that is left. In these lessons, we will say a word. We will delete or take away the first sound and say what is left.

### I DO:

I will show you how we can delete or take away the first sound from a word and say what is left.

| peach | T: Watch me. When I say peach, and delete or take away /p/, what's left is, each. |
|-------|---------------------------------------------------------------------------------|
| damp  | T: The word is damp. When I delete or take away /d/, what's left is amp.          |

### WE DO:

Let's try some words together. I will say a word. You will repeat the word. We will delete or take away a sound and say what is left.

| hit  | T: Say, hit. <br> T & S: hit <br> T: Without /h/, what's left is? <br> T & S: it |
|------|---------------------------------------------------------------------------------|
| coat | T: Say, coat <br> T & S: coat <br> T: Without /k/, what's left is? <br> T & S: oat |

### YOU DO:

Now it is your turn. I will say a word. You will repeat the word. I will tell you the sound to delete and you will tell me what is left.

| SAY: | WITHOUT: | WHAT'S LEFT IS: |
|------|----------|-----------------|
| can  | /k/      | an              |
| send | /s/      | end             |
| bake | /b/      | ache            |

*Say sound, not letter name

**DELETING AND MOTION:**

Hold 2 open palms in front of you. Teacher's right hand is the first sound, left hand is the rest of the word. Pull your right hand away when deleting the first sound, and show what part remains with your left hand.

### TEACHER TIPS:

① The teacher can use a hand motion to show what part of a word is being adding or deleted. The teachers right hand/palm is the initial sound and left palm/hand is the rime or word family.

② ▮ ▮ Felt squares can be used to represent the sounds and provide a visual anchor for learners.

# Adding & Deleting Initial Phonemes

LESSON FOCUS: When we say a word or a word part, we can add a sound at the beginning to make a new word.

⇨ Lesson 1: Adding Initial Phonemes

Teacher Directions: I will say a word/word part. You will repeat the word. We will add a sound at the beginning and you will tell me the new word.

Student Response: Students repeat the first word aloud, then say the new word with the initial phoneme the teacher provided.

| SAY: | ADD /*/ AT THE BEGINNING | THE WORD IS: |
|---|---|---|
| and | /h/ | hand |
| oil | /r/ | royal |
| aid | /m/ | made |

| SAY: | ADD /*/ AT THE BEGINNING | THE WORD IS: |
|---|---|---|
| ink | /th/ | think |
| old | /b/ | bold |
| ouch | /k/ | couch |

✋ ADDING HAND MOTION: Teacher holds left palm out to show the word/word part. Add the first sound with right hand and lightly clap hands together for the whole word.

🍎 TEACHER TIP: If students are struggling to create new word, you can scaffold support by saying the onset and rime, and then blend the two together. Example: /h/-/and/, hand.

LESSON FOCUS: When we hear whole words, we can take a sound away and say what is left. Sometimes taking away a sound makes a new word, and other times, it is just a word part that is left.

⇨ Lesson 1: Deleting Initial Phonemes

Teacher Directions: I will say a word. You will repeat the word. We will take away or delete the first sound and you will tell me what is left.

Student response: Students repeat the word aloud, then say the new word without the initial phoneme.

| WHOLE WORD: | WITHOUT | WHAT'S LEFT IS: |
|---|---|---|
| pout | /p/ | out |
| bend | /b/ | end |
| chow | /ch/ | ow |

| WHOLE WORD: | WITHOUT | WHAT'S LEFT IS: |
|---|---|---|
| learn | /l/ | earn |
| howl | /h/ | owl |
| rant | /r/ | ant |

✋ DELETING HAND MOTION: Hold 2 open palms in front of you. Teacher's right hand is the first sound, left hand is the rest of the word. Pull your right hand away when deleting the first sound, and show what part remains with your left hand.

🍎 TEACHER TIP: Remember to say the sound, not the letter name, when deleting the phoneme from the word.

# Adding & Deleting Initial Phonemes

**LESSON FOCUS:** When we say a word or a word part, we can add a sound at the beginning to make a new word.

## Lesson 2: Adding Initial Phonemes

Teacher Directions: I will say a word. You will repeat the word. We will add a sound at the beginning and you will tell me the new word.

Student Response: Students repeat the first word aloud, then say the new word with the initial phoneme the teacher provided.

| SAY: | ADD /*/ AT THE BEGINNING | THE WORD IS: | SAY: | ADD /*/ AT THE BEGINNING | THE WORD IS: |
|------|--------------------------|--------------|------|--------------------------|--------------|
| own | /t/ | tone | out | /sh/ | shout |
| older | /sh/ | shoulder | under | /th/ | thunder |
| ink | /w/ | wink | ache | /sh/ | shake |

**ADDING HAND MOTION:** Teacher holds left palm out to show the word/word part. Add the first sound with right hand and lightly clap hands together for the whole word.

**TEACHER TIP:** If students are struggling to create new word, you can scaffold support by saying the onset and rime, and then blend the two together. Example: /w/-/ink/, wink.

**LESSON FOCUS:** When we hear whole words, we can take a sound away and say what is left. Sometimes taking away a sound makes a new word, and other times, it is just a word part that is left.

## Lesson 2: Deleting Initial Phonemes

Teacher Directions: I will say a word. You will repeat the word. We will take away or delete the first sound and you will tell me what is left.

Student Response: Students repeat the word aloud, then say the new word without the initial phoneme.

| WHOLE WORD: | WITHOUT | WHAT'S LEFT IS: | WHOLE WORD: | WITHOUT | WHAT'S LEFT IS: |
|-------------|---------|-----------------|-------------|---------|-----------------|
| told | /t/ | old | bear | /b/ | air |
| rhyme | /r/ | ime/I'm | charm | /ch/ | arm |
| cheese | /ch/ | ease | shark | /sh/ | ark |

**DELETING HAND MOTION:** Hold 2 open palms in front of you. Teacher's right hand is the first sound, left hand is the rest of the word. Pull your right hand away when deleting the first sound, and show what part remains with your left hand.

**TEACHER TIP:** Remember to say the sound, not the letter name, when deleting the phoneme from the word.

# Adding & Deleting Initial Phonemes

**LESSON FOCUS:** When we say a word or a word part, we can add a sound at the beginning to make a new word.

## Lesson 3: Adding Initial Phonemes

Teacher Directions: I will say a word/word part. You will repeat the word. We will add a sound at the beginning and you will tell me the new word.

Student Response: Students repeat the first word/word part aloud, then say the new word with the initial phoneme the teacher provided.

| SAY: | ADD /*/ AT THE BEGINNING | THE WORD IS: |
|---|---|---|
| ing | /th/ | thing |
| alk | /w/ | walk |
| unk | /j/ | junk |

| SAY: | ADD /*/ AT THE BEGINNING | THE WORD IS: |
|---|---|---|
| oast | /g/ | ghost |
| ood | /k/ | could |
| ang | /s/ | sang |

**ADDING HAND MOTION:** Teacher holds left palm out to show the word/word part. Add the first sound with right hand and lightly clap hands together for the whole word.

**TEACHER TIP:** If students are struggling to create new word, you can scaffold support by saying the onset and rime, and then blend the two together. Example: /th/-/ing/, thing.

**LESSON FOCUS:** When we hear whole words, we can take a sound away and say what is left. Sometimes taking away a sound makes a new word, and other times, it is just a word part that is left.

## Lesson 3: Deleting Initial Phonemes

Teacher Directions: I will say a word. You will repeat the word. We will take away or delete the first sound and you will tell me what is left.

Student Response: Students repeat the word aloud, then say the new word without the initial phoneme.

| WHOLE WORD: | WITHOUT | WHAT'S LEFT IS: |
|---|---|---|
| point | /p/ | oint |
| west | /w/ | est |
| hold | /h/ | old |

| WHOLE WORD: | WITHOUT | WHAT'S LEFT IS: |
|---|---|---|
| soar | /s/ | oar |
| feast | /f/ | east |
| burn | /b/ | urn |

**DELETING HAND MOTION:** Hold 2 open palms in front of you. Teacher's right hand is the first sound, left hand is the rest of the word. Pull your right hand away when deleting the first sound, and show what part remains with your left hand.

**TEACHER TIP:** Remember to say the sound, not the letter name, when deleting the phoneme from the word.

# Adding & Deleting Initial Phonemes

**LESSON FOCUS:** When we say a word or a word part, we can add a sound at the beginning to make a new word.

⇨ Lesson 4 Adding Initial Phonemes

Teacher Directions: I will say a word/word part. You will repeat the word. We will add a sound at the beginning and you will tell me the new word.

Student Response: Students repeat the first word/word part aloud, then say the new word with the initial phoneme the teacher provided.

| SAY: | ADD /*/ AT THE BEGINNING | THE WORD IS: | | SAY: | ADD /*/ AT THE BEGINNING | THE WORD IS: |
|------|--------------------------|--------------|---|------|--------------------------|--------------|
| amp  | /k/ | camp | | oom  | /z/ | zoom  |
| elt  | /b/ | belt | | ear  | /d/ | dear  |
| unt  | /h/ | hunt | | oise | /n/ | noise |

✋ **ADDING HAND MOTION:** Teacher holds left palm out to show the word/word part. Add the first sound with right hand and lightly clap hands together for the whole word.

🍎 **TEACHER TIP:** If students are struggling to create new word, you can scaffold support by saying the onset and rime, and then blend the two together. Example: /b/-/elt/, belt.

**LESSON FOCUS:** When we hear whole words, we can take a sound away and say what is left. Sometimes taking away a sound makes a new word, and other times, it is just a word part that is left.

⇨ Lesson 4: Deleting Initial Phonemes

Teacher Directions: I will say a word. You will repeat the word. We will take away or delete the first sound and you will tell me what is left.

Student Response: Students repeat the word aloud, then say the new word without the initial phoneme.

| WHOLE WORD: | WITHOUT | WHAT'S LEFT IS: | | WHOLE WORD: | WITHOUT | WHAT'S LEFT IS: |
|-------------|---------|-----------------|---|-------------|---------|-----------------|
| pause  | /p/  | ause | | build   | /b/  | ïld  |
| choice | /ch/ | oice | | mask    | /m/  | ask  |
| sound  | /s/  | ound | | thought | /th/ | ought |

✋ **DELETING HAND MOTION:** Hold 2 open palms in front of you. Teacher's right hand is the first sound, left hand is the rest of the word. Pull your right hand away when deleting the first sound, and show what part remains with your left hand.

🍎 **TEACHER TIP:** Remember to say the sound, not the letter name, when deleting the phoneme from the word.

# Adding Initial Phonemes

LESSON FOCUS: We can make a new word by adding a sound to the beginning to create a consonant blend. In these lessons, I will say a word and we will add a sound at the beginning to make a word that begins with a consonant blend.

**I WILL MODEL THIS FOR YOU; WATCH ME.**

When I say, low and add /s/ at the beginning, the word is: /s/-/low/, slow.

Let's try this one together and see if we can add the initial sound and say just the new word:

Say, lap. Add /f/ at the beginning and the word is? Flap.

⊕ **Lesson 5: Adding Initial Phonemes**

Teacher Directions: I will say a word. You will repeat the word. We will add a sound at the beginning and you will tell me the new word.

Student Response: Students repeat the first word aloud, then say the new word with the initial phoneme the teacher provided.

| SAY: | ADD /*/ AT THE BEGINNING | THE WORD IS: |
|------|--------------------------|--------------|
| red | /b/ | bread |
| team | /s/ | steam |
| rate | /g/ | great |

| SAY: | ADD /*/ AT THE BEGINNING | THE WORD IS: |
|------|--------------------------|--------------|
| light | /f/ | flight |
| row | /k/ | crow |
| ledge | /p/ | pledge |

🖐 ADDING HAND MOTION: Teacher holds left palm out to show the word/word part. Add the first sound with right hand and lightly clap hands together for the whole word.

🍎

**TEACHER TIPS:**

① If students struggle to add the initial sound, use felt or counters to represent the sounds. Start with two pieces of felt: one small piece to represent the first sound and one larger piece to represent the rest of the word. Add a small piece to the beginning when adding the initial sound.

▮ ▮ ▬

② If students are struggling to create the blend, you can scaffold support by saying the first sound and the word apart, and then blend together. Example: /s/-/low/, slow

# Deleting Initial Phonemes

LESSON FOCUS: When we hear whole words, we can take a sound away and say what is left. In these lessons, we will delete or take away the first sound from a consonant blend.

**I WILL MODEL THIS FOR YOU; WATCH ME.**

When I say, slow and I delete only the first sound, /s/, what's left is low.

Let's try this one together and see if we can delete the initial sound and say what is left:

Say, flap. Without /f/, what's left is? lap

⟶ Lesson 5: Deleting Initial Phonemes

Teacher Directions: I will say a word. You will repeat the word. We will take away or delete only the first sound and you will tell me what is left.

Student Response: Students repeat the word aloud, then say the new word without the initial phoneme.

| WHOLE WORD: | WITHOUT | WHAT'S LEFT IS: |
| --- | --- | --- |
| frail | /f/ | rail |
| broom | /b/ | room |
| cloud | /k/ | loud |

| WHOLE WORD: | WITHOUT | WHAT'S LEFT IS: |
| --- | --- | --- |
| style | /s/ | tile |
| pry | /p/ | rye |
| glow | /g/ | low |

✋ DELETING HAND MOTION: Hold 2 open palms in front of you. Teacher's right hand is the first sound, left hand is the rest of the word. Pull your right hand away when deleting the first sound, and show what part remains with your left hand.

🍎

### TEACHER TIP:

If students struggle to delete the initial sound, use felt or counters to represent the sounds. Start with three pieces of felt: two small pieces to represent the blend and one larger piece to represent the rest of the word. Remove the first piece of felt when deleting the initial sound to show what is left.

# Adding & Deleting Initial Phonemes

LESSON FOCUS: We can make a new word by adding a sound to the beginning of a word to create a consonant blend. In these lessons, I will say a word and we will add a sound at the beginning to make a word that begins with a consonant blend.

## Lesson 6: Adding Initial Phonemes

Teacher Directions: I will say a word. You will repeat the word. We will add a sound at the beginning and you will tell me the new word.

Student Response: Students repeat the first word aloud, then say the new word with the initial phoneme the teacher provided.

| SAY: | ADD /*/ AT THE BEGINNING | THE WORD IS: | SAY: | ADD /*/ AT THE BEGINNING | THE WORD IS: |
|------|--------------------------|--------------|------|--------------------------|--------------|
| lamp | /k/ | clamp | lock | /b/ | block |
| root | /f/ | fruit | rain | /g/ | grain |
| port | /s/ | sport | rinse | /p/ | prince |

ADDING HAND MOTION: Teacher holds left palm out to show the word part. Add the first sound with right hand and lightly clap hands together for the whole word.

LESSON FOCUS: When we hear whole words, we can take a sound away and say what is left. In these lessons, we will delete or take away away the first sound.

## Lesson 6: Deleting Initial Phonemes

Teacher Directions: I will say a word. You will repeat the word. We will take away or delete only the first sound and you will tell me what is left.

Student Response: Students repeat the word aloud, then say the new word without the initial phoneme.

| WHOLE WORD: | WITHOUT | WHAT'S LEFT IS: | WHOLE WORD: | WITHOUT | WHAT'S LEFT IS: |
|-------------|---------|-----------------|-------------|---------|-----------------|
| grow | /g/ | row | floss | /f/ | loss |
| blink | /b/ | link | climb | /k/ | lime |
| prize | /p/ | rise | snap | /s/ | nap |

DELETING HAND MOTION: Hold 2 open palms in front of you. Teacher's right hand is the first sound, left hand is the rest of the word. Pull your right hand away when deleting the first sound, and show what part remains with your left hand.

### TEACHER TIP:

If students struggle to delete the initial sound, use felt or counters to represent the sounds. Start with three pieces of felt: two small pieces to represent the blend and one larger piece to represent the rest of the word. Remove the first piece of felt when deleting the initial sound to show what is left.

# Adding & Deleting Initial Phonemes

**LESSON FOCUS:** We can make a new word by adding a sound to the beginning of a word to create a consonant blend. In these lessons, I will say a word and we will add a sound at the beginning to make a word that begins with a consonant blend.

## Lesson 7: Adding Initial Phonemes

Teacher Directions: I will say a word. You will repeat the word. We will add a sound at the beginning and you will tell me the new word.

Student Response: Students repeat the first word aloud, then say the new word with the initial phoneme the teacher provided.

| SAY: | ADD /*/ AT THE BEGINNING | THE WORD IS: |
| --- | --- | --- |
| table | /s/ | stable |
| rink | /sh/ | shrink |
| rises | /p/ | prizes |

| SAY: | ADD /*/ AT THE BEGINNING | THE WORD IS: |
| --- | --- | --- |
| rumble | /k/ | crumble |
| ringing | /b/ | bringing |
| rate | /f/ | freight |

**ADDING HAND MOTION:** Teacher holds left palm out to show the word. Add the first sound with right hand and lightly clap hands together for the whole word.

**TEACHER TIP:** Scaffolded support can be provided by saying, /b-ring/, bring, or using visuals to represent the 2 sounds of the blend.

**LESSON FOCUS:** When we hear whole words, we can take a sound away and say what is left. In these lessons, we will delete or take away away the first sound.

## Lesson 7: Deleting Initial Phonemes

Teacher Directions: I will say a word. You will repeat the word. We will take away or delete the first sound and you will tell me what is left.

Student Response: Students repeat the word aloud, then say the new word without the initial phoneme.

| WHOLE WORD: | WITHOUT | WHAT'S LEFT IS: |
| --- | --- | --- |
| thread | /th/ | red |
| slump | /s/ | lump |
| snapping | /s/ | napping |

| WHOLE WORD: | WITHOUT | WHAT'S LEFT IS: |
| --- | --- | --- |
| player | /p/ | layer |
| ground | /g/ | round |
| swallow | /s/ | wallow |

*/*/ sound, not letter name*

**DELETING HAND MOTION:** Hold 2 open palms in front of you. Teacher's right hand is the first sound, left hand is the rest of the word. Pull your right hand away when deleting the first sound, and show what part remains with your left hand.

**TEACHER TIP:** Segment the two sounds of the blend: /s/-/t/-able. When we delete /s/, what's left is /t/-able, table

# Adding & Deleting Initial Phonemes

LESSON FOCUS: We can make a new word by adding a sound to the beginning of a word to create a consonant blend. In these lessons, I will say a word and we will add a sound at the beginning to make a word that begins with a consonant blend.

## Lesson 8: Adding Initial Phonemes

Teacher Directions: I will say a word part. You will repeat the word. We will add a sound at the beginning and you will tell me the new word.

Student Response: Students repeat the first word aloud, then say the new word with the initial phoneme the teacher provided.

| SAY: | ADD /*/ AT THE BEGINNING | THE WORD IS: |
|---|---|---|
| platter | /s/ | splatter |
| rink | /b/ | brink |
| laying | /p/ | playing |

| SAY: | ADD /*/ AT THE BEGINNING | THE WORD IS: |
|---|---|---|
| leaner | /k/ | cleaner |
| round | /g/ | ground |
| writer | /b/ | brighter |

✋ ADDING HAND MOTION: Teacher holds left palm out to show the word/word part. Add the first sound with right hand and lightly clap hands together for the whole word.

LESSON FOCUS: When we hear whole words, we can take a sound away and say what is left. In these lessons, we will delete or take away away the first sound.

## Lesson 8: Deleting Initial Phonemes

Teacher Directions: I will say a word. You will repeat the word. We will take away or delete the first sound and you will tell me what is left.

Student Response: Students repeat the word aloud, then say the new word without the initial phoneme.

| WHOLE WORD: | WITHOUT | WHAT'S LEFT IS: |
|---|---|---|
| president | /p/ | resident |
| blend | /b/ | lend |
| slime | /s/ | lime |

| WHOLE WORD: | WITHOUT | WHAT'S LEFT IS: |
|---|---|---|
| greed | /g/ | reed |
| flyer | /f/ | lyer (liar) |
| smother | /s/ | mother |

✋ DELETING HAND MOTION: Hold 2 open palms in front of you. Teacher's right hand is the first sound, left hand is the rest of the word. Pull your right hand away when deleting the first sound, and show what part remains with your left hand.

🍎 TEACHER TIP: If students struggle to add or delete the initial sound, use felt or counters to represent the sounds. Start with two pieces and place a piece of felt at the beginning when adding the initial sound or pull away the first felt piece when deleting the initial sound of the blend.

# Adding & Deleting Initial Phonemes

**LESSON FOCUS:** We can make a new word by adding a sound to the beginning of a word to create a consonant blend. In these lessons, I will say a word and we will add a sound at the beginning to make a word that begins with a consonant blend.

## Lesson 9: Adding Initial Phonemes

Teacher Directions: I will say a word part. You will repeat it. It may be a nonsense word. We will add a sound at the beginning, and you will tell me the new word.

Student Response: Students repeat the first word aloud, then say the new word with the initial phoneme the teacher provided.

| SAY: | ADD /*/ AT THE BEGINNING | THE WORD IS: |
|------|--------------------------|--------------|
| tarch | /s/ | starch |
| lŏwn | /k/ | clown |
| rŏnze | /b/ | bronze |

| SAY: | ADD /*/ AT THE BEGINNING | THE WORD IS: |
|------|--------------------------|--------------|
| lānk | /p/ | plank |
| litch | /g/ | glitch |
| resh | /f/ | fresh |

**ADDING HAND MOTION:** Teacher holds left palm out to show the word/word part. Add the first sound with right hand and lightly clap hands together for the whole word.

**TEACHER TIP:** Scaffolded support can be provided by saying, /s-niff/, sniff, or using visuals to represent the 2 sounds of the blend.

**LESSON FOCUS:** When we hear whole words, we can take a sound away and say what is left. In these lessons, we will delete or take away away the first sound.

## Lesson 9: Deleting Initial Phonemes

Teacher Directions: I will say a word. You will repeat the word. We will take away or delete the first sound and you will tell me what is left. When we take a sound away, what is left may be a word part and not a real word.

Student Response: Students repeat the word aloud, then say the new word/word part without the initial phoneme.

| WHOLE WORD: | WITHOUT | WHAT'S LEFT IS: |
|-------------|---------|-----------------|
| proud | /p/ | rŏud |
| smooth | /s/ | mooth* |
| glance | /g/ | lance |

| WHOLE WORD: | WITHOUT | WHAT'S LEFT IS: |
|-------------|---------|-----------------|
| sneak | /s/ | neak |
| blonde | /b/ | lŏnde |
| fringe | /f/ | rĭnge |

**DELETING HAND MOTION:** Hold 2 open palms in front of you. Teacher's right hand is the first sound, left hand is the rest of the word. Pull your right hand away when deleting the first sound, and show what part remains with your left hand.

**TEACHER TIP:** Remind students to delete only the first sound from a blend, not both sounds of the blend.

# Adding & Deleting Initial Phonemes

**LESSON FOCUS:** We can make a new word by adding a sound to the beginning of a word to create a consonant blend. In these lessons, I will say a word and we will add a sound at the beginning to make a word that begins with a consonant blend.

⊛ Lesson 10: Adding Initial Phonemes

Teacher Directions: I will say a word part. You will repeat it. It may be a nonsense word. We will add a sound at the beginning, and you will tell me the new word.

Student Response: Students repeat the first word/word part aloud, then say the new word with the initial phoneme the teacher provided.

| SAY: | ADD /*/ AT THE BEGINNING | THE WORD IS: | | SAY: | ADD /*/ AT THE BEGINNING | THE WORD IS: |
|------|--------------------------|--------------|---|------|--------------------------|--------------|
| laze | /b/ | blaze | | lum | /p/ | plum |
| rand | /g/ | grand | | rŏwl | /g/ | growl |
| tew | /s/ | stew | | poon | /s/ | spoon |

✋ **ADDING HAND MOTION:** Teacher holds left palm out to show the word/word part. Add the first sound with right hand and lightly clap hands together for the whole word.

**LESSON FOCUS:** When we hear whole words, we can take a sound away and say what is left. In these lessons, we will delete or take away away the first sound.

⊛ Lesson 10: Deleting Initial Phonemes

Teacher Directions: I will say a word. You will repeat the word. We will take away or delete the first sound and you will tell me what is left. When we take a sound away, what is left may be a word part and not a real word.

Student Response: Students repeat the word aloud, then say the new word without the initial phoneme.

| WHOLE WORD: | WITHOUT | WHAT'S LEFT IS: | | WHOLE WORD: | WITHOUT | WHAT'S LEFT IS: |
|-------------|---------|-----------------|---|-------------|---------|-----------------|
| spring | /s/ | pring | | grizzly | /g/ | rizzly |
| twelve | /t/ | wĕlve | | blanket | /b/ | lānket |
| plastic | /p/ | lastic | | fraction | /f/ | răction |

✋ **DELETING HAND MOTION:** Hold 2 open palms in front of you. Teacher's right hand is the first sound, left hand is the rest of the word. Pull your right hand away when deleting the first sound, and show what part remains with your left hand.

🍎 **TEACHER TIP:** If students struggle to add or delete the initial sound, use felt or counters to represent the sounds. Start with two pieces and place a piece of felt at the beginning when adding the initial sound or pull away the first felt piece when deleting the initial sound of the blend.

▮▮ ▮

# Adding Initial Phonemes

We have worked on many lessons with adding a sound to a word or word part to make a new word. Today, you will show me what you have learned.

Teacher Administration Directions: I will say a word part. You will say it back to me. I will tell you a sound to add at the beginning. You will tell me the new word.

Recording Directions: Record incorrect responses in the Student Response column. If correct, mark with a check or +

Student Name: _____     Date: _____

|    | WORD:    | ADD /*/ AT THE BEGINNING: | THE WORD IS: | STUDENT RESPONSE: |
|----|----------|---------------------------|--------------|-------------------|
| 1  | in       | /sh/                      | shin         |                   |
| 2  | room     | /g/                       | groom        |                   |
| 3  | low      | /b/                       | blow         |                   |
| 4  | only     | /l/                       | lonely       |                   |
| 5  | platter  | /s/                       | splatter     |                   |
| 6  | ever     | /n/                       | never        |                   |
| 7  | rib      | /k/                       | crib         |                   |
| 8  | under    | /th/                      | thunder      |                   |
| 9  | table    | /s/                       | stable       |                   |
| 10 | rice     | /p/                       | price        |                   |

Score: ____ /10

**SCORING GUIDE:**

0-5 correct:  Review Adding Initial Phonemes Lessons 1-10

6-8 correct:  Review Adding Initial Phonemes Lessons 6-10

9-10 correct:  Move on to Adding Final Phonemes Lessons 11-20

# Deleting Initial Phonemes

We have worked on many lessons with deleting a sound in a word to say what is left. Today, you will show me what you have learned.

Teacher Administration Directions: I will say a word. You will say it back to me. I will tell you a sound to delete or take away from the beginning. You will tell me what is left.

Recording Directions: Record incorrect responses in the Student Response column. If correct, mark with a check or +

Student Name: _____  Date: _____

|  | WORD: | WITHOUT /*/ | WHAT'S LEFT IS: | STUDENT RESPONSE: |
|---|---|---|---|---|
| 1 | crime | /k/ | rhyme | |
| 2 | swipe | /s/ | wipe | |
| 3 | table | /t/ | able | |
| 4 | bounces | /b/ | ounces | |
| 5 | plate | /p/ | late | |
| 6 | shape | /sh/ | ape | |
| 7 | bridge | /b/ | ridge | |
| 8 | flash | /f/ | lash | |
| 9 | sweater | /s/ | wetter | |
| 10 | glove | /g/ | love | |
| | | | | Score:     /10 |

**SCORING GUIDE:**

0-5 correct:  Review Deleting Initial Phonemes Lessons 1-10

6-8 correct:  Review Deleting Initial Phonemes Lessons 6-10

9-10 correct:  Move on to Deleting Final Phonemes Lessons 11-20

# Anchor Lesson: Adding Final Phonemes

LESSON FOCUS: We have been practicing adding sounds to the beginning of a word. In these lessons, we will make new words by adding a sound at the end of a word or word part.

## I DO:

I will show you how we can add a sound to the end of a word or word part to make a new word.

| start | T: Watch me. When I say the word, star and add /t/ at the end, the word is /star/ - /t/, start. I said the two parts and blended them together to make a new word. We can do that quickly, without repeating the parts. Listen: Star add /t/ at the end, and the word is start. |
|-------|---|
| plate | T: The word is play. When I add /t/ at the end, the word is play - /t/, plate. |

## WE DO:

Let's try some words together. I will say a word. You will repeat the word. We will add a sound at the end and say the new word.

| shelf | T: Say, shell |
|-------|---|
|       | T & S: shell |
|       | T: Add /f/ at the end, and the word is? |
|       | T & S: shelf |
| storm | T: Say, store |
|       | T & S: store |
|       | T: Add /m/ at the end, and the word is? |
|       | T & S: storm |

## YOU DO:

Now it's your turn. I will say a word/word part. You will say it back to me. I will tell you a sound to add at the end. You will tell me the new word.

| SAY: | ADD /*/ AT THE END | THE WORD IS: |
|------|---------------------|--------------|
| too | /th/ | tooth |
| pay | /l/ | pail |
| for | /s/ | force |

✋ ADDING HAND MOTION:

Teacher holds left palm out to show the word/word part. Add the first sound with right hand and lightly clap hands together for the whole word.

🍎

TEACHER TIP:

If students struggle, provide support. Repeat the two parts of the word and blend together. Example: The word is car. When I add /d/ at the end, the word is /car/ - /d/, card.

# Anchor Lesson: Deleting Final Phonemes

LESSON FOCUS: We have been practicing deleting sounds from the beginning of a word. We can also make new words by deleting a sound at the end of a word. In these lessons, we will say a word. We will delete or take away the last or final sound and say what is left.

## I DO:

I will show you how we can delete or take away the final sound from a word and say what is left.

| feet | T: Watch me. When I say the word, feet and delete /t/ from the end, what is left is fee. Listen, /fee/ - /t/, without /t/, what's left is fee. |
| farm | T: Listen: The word is farm. Without /m/, what's left is far. |

## WE DO:

Let's try some words together. I will say a word. You will repeat the word. We will delete or take away the final sound and say what is left.

| plate | T: Say, plate |
| | T & S: plate |
| | T: Without /t/, what's left is? |
| | T & S: play |
| stay | T: Say stake |
| | T & S: stake |
| | T: Without /k/, what's left is? |
| | T & S: stay |

## YOU DO:

Now it's your turn. I will say a word. You will say it back to me. I will tell you the sound to delete, and you will tell me what is left.

| SAY: | WITHOUT | WHAT'S LEFT IS: |
|---|---|---|
| course | /s/ | core |
| shirt | /t/ | sure |
| teach | /ch/ | tea |

**DELETING AND MOTION:**

Hold 2 open palms in front of you. Teacher's right hand is the first sound, left hand is the rest of the word. Pull your right hand away when deleting the first sound, and show what part remains with your left hand.

**TEACHER TIPS:**

1. If students struggle, provide support: We can segment the word into 2 parts: /core/ - /s/. When we delete the final sound /s/, what's left is core.

2. /*/ say sound, not letter name

# Adding & Deleting Final Phonemes

**LESSON FOCUS:** When we say a word or a word part, we can add a sound at the end to make a new word.

⇨ Lesson 11: Adding Final Phonemes

Teacher Directions: I will say a word. You will say it back to me. We will add a sound at the end and you will tell me the new word.

Student Response: Students repeat the first word aloud, then say the new word with the final phoneme the teacher provided.

| SAY: | ADD /*/ AT THE END | THE WORD IS: |
|------|------|------|
| high | /k/ | hike |
| way | /t/ | wait |
| row | /z/ | rose |

| SAY: | ADD /*/ AT THE END | THE WORD IS: |
|------|------|------|
| bar | /n/ | barn |
| so | /p/ | soap |
| knee | /t/ | neat |

✋ **ADDING HAND MOTION:** Teacher holds right palm to show word. Add the final sound with left hand and lightly clap hands together for the whole word.

**LESSON FOCUS:** When we hear whole words, we can take a sound away and say what is left. Sometimes taking away a sound makes a new word, and other times, it is just a word part that is left.

⇨ Lesson 11: Deleting Final Phonemes

Teacher Directions: I will say a word. You will say the word back to me. We will take away or delete the final sound and you will tell me what is left.

Student Response: Students repeat the word aloud, then say the new word without the final phoneme.

| WHOLE WORD: | WITHOUT | WHAT'S LEFT IS: |
|------|------|------|
| seat | /t/ | see |
| nose | /z/ | no |
| wave | /v/ | way |

| WHOLE WORD: | WITHOUT | WHAT'S LEFT IS: |
|------|------|------|
| fork | /k/ | for |
| robe | /b/ | row |
| weed | /d/ | we |

✋ **DELETING HAND MOTION:** Hold 2 palms out in front of you. Teacher's left hand is the final sound, right hand is the rest of the word. Pull left hand away when deleting the final phoneme, and show what part remains with your right hand.

🍎

**TEACHER TIP:**

/*/ Always add or delete the sound, not the letter name

# Adding & Deleting Final Phonemes

**LESSON FOCUS:** When we say a word or a word part, we can add a sound at the end to make a new word.

⊜ **Lesson 12: Adding Final Phonemes**

Teacher Directions: I will say a word. You will say it back to me. We will add a sound at the end and you will tell me the new word.

Student Response: Students repeat the first word aloud, then say the new word with the final phoneme the teacher provided.

| SAY: | ADD /*/ AT THE END | THE WORD IS: |
|---|---|---|
| rye | /s/ | rice |
| see | /k/ | seek |
| pay | /d/ | paid |

| SAY: | ADD /*/ AT THE END | THE WORD IS: |
|---|---|---|
| why | /z/ | wise |
| poor | /ch/ | porch |
| lie | /t/ | light |

✋ **ADDING HAND MOTION:** Teacher holds right palm to show word. Add the final sound with left hand and lightly clap hands together for the whole word.

**LESSON FOCUS:** When we hear whole words, we can take a sound away and say what is left. Sometimes taking away a sound makes a new word, and other times, it is just a word part that is left.

⊜ **Lesson 12: Deleting Final Phonemes**

Teacher Directions: I will say a word. You will say the word back to me. We will take away or delete the final sound and you will tell me what is left.

Student Response: Students repeat the word aloud, then say the new word without the final phoneme.

| WHOLE WORD: | WITHOUT | WHAT'S LEFT IS: |
|---|---|---|
| keep | /p/ | key |
| soak | /k/ | so |
| short | /t/ | shore |

| WHOLE WORD: | WITHOUT | WHAT'S LEFT IS: |
|---|---|---|
| feed | /d/ | fee |
| haze | /z/ | hay |
| lace | /s/ | lay |

✋ **DELETING HAND MOTION:** Hold 2 palms out in front of you. Teacher's left hand is the final sound, right hand is the rest of the word. Pull left hand away when deleting the final phoneme, and show what part remains with your right hand.

**TEACHER TIP:**

/*/ Always add or delete the sound, not the letter name

# Adding & Deleting Final Phonemes

**LESSON FOCUS:** When we say a word or a word part, we can add a sound at the end to make a new word.

⇨ Lesson 13: Adding Final Phonemes

Teacher Directions: I will say a word. You will say it back to me. We will add a sound at the end and you will tell me the new word.

Student Response: Students repeat the first word aloud, then say the new word with the final phoneme the teacher provided.

| SAY: | ADD /*/ AT THE END | THE WORD IS: |
|------|--------------------|--------------|
| fly  | /t/ | flight |
| stay | /k/ | steak |
| pry  | /d/ | pride |

| SAY: | ADD /*/ AT THE END | THE WORD IS: |
|------|--------------------|--------------|
| grew | /p/ | group |
| play | /n/ | plane |
| glow | /t/ | gloat |

✋ **ADDING HAND MOTION:** Teacher holds right palm to show word. Add the final sound with left hand and lightly clap hands together for the whole word.

**LESSON FOCUS:** When we hear whole words, we can take a sound away and say what is left. Sometimes taking away a sound makes a new word, and other times, it is just a word part that is left.

⇨ Lesson 13: Deleting Final Phonemes

Teacher Directions: I will say a word. You will say the word back to me. We will take away or delete the final sound and you will tell me what is left.

Student Response: Students repeat the word aloud, then say the new word without the final phoneme.

| WHOLE WORD: | WITHOUT | WHAT'S LEFT IS: |
|-------------|---------|-----------------|
| great | /t/ | gray |
| team  | /m/ | tea |
| stage | /j/ | stay |

| WHOLE WORD: | WITHOUT | WHAT'S LEFT IS: |
|-------------|---------|-----------------|
| freeze | /z/ | free |
| grown  | /n/ | grow |
| pace   | /s/ | pay |

✋ **DELETING HAND MOTION:** Hold 2 palms out in front of you. Teacher's left hand is the final sound, right hand is the rest of the word. Pull left hand away when deleting the final phoneme, and show what part remains with your right hand.

**TEACHER TIP:**

/*/ Always add or delete the sound, not the letter name

# Adding & Deleting Final Phonemes

**LESSON FOCUS:** When we say a word or a word part, we can add a sound at the end to make a new word.

⇨ Lesson 14: Adding Final Phonemes

Teacher Directions: I will say a word. You will say it back to me. We will add a sound at the end and you will tell me the new word.

Student Response: Students repeat the first word aloud, then say the new word with the final phoneme the teacher provided.

| SAY: | ADD /*/ AT THE END | THE WORD IS: | SAY: | ADD /*/ AT THE END | THE WORD IS: |
|------|-----|-----|-----|-----|-----|
| boar | /d/ | board | for | /k/ | fork |
| mar | /ch/ | march | sore | /t/ | sort |
| were | /m/ | worm | paw | /n/ | pawn |

🖐 **ADDING HAND MOTION:** Teacher holds right palm to show word. Add the final sound with left hand and lightly clap hands together for the whole word.

**LESSON FOCUS:** When we hear whole words, we can take a sound away and say what is left. Sometimes taking away a sound makes a new word, and other times, it is just a word part that is left.

⇨ Lesson 14: Deleting Final Phonemes

Teacher Directions: I will say a word. You will say the word back to me. We will take away or delete the final sound and you will tell me what is left.

Student Response: Students repeat the word aloud, then say the new word without the final phoneme.

| WHOLE WORD: | WITHOUT | WHAT'S LEFT IS: | WHOLE WORD: | WITHOUT | WHAT'S LEFT IS: |
|------|-----|-----|-----|-----|-----|
| lamp | /p/ | lamb | meant | /t/ | men |
| pinch | /ch/ | pin | ramp | /p/ | ram |
| gold | /d/ | goal | heard | /d/ | her |

🖐 **DELETING HAND MOTION:** Hold 2 palms out in front of you. Teacher's left hand is the final sound, right hand is the rest of the word. Pull left hand away when deleting the final phoneme, and show what part remains with your right hand.

**TEACHER TIP:**

/*/ Always add or delete the sound, not the letter name

# Adding & Deleting Final Phonemes

**LESSON FOCUS:** When we say a word or a word part, we can add a sound at the end to make a new word.

⊕ Lesson 15: Adding Final Phonemes

Teacher Directions: I will say a word. You will say it back to me. We will add a sound at the end and you will tell me the new word.

Student Response: Students repeat the first word aloud, then say the new word with the final phoneme the teacher provided.

| SAY: | ADD /*/ AT THE END | THE WORD IS: |
|------|------|------|
| clam | /p/ | clamp |
| store | /k/ | stork |
| fine | /d/ | find |

| SAY: | ADD /*/ AT THE END | THE WORD IS: |
|------|------|------|
| chess | /t/ | chest |
| core | /d/ | cord |
| gas | /p/ | gasp |

✋ **ADDING HAND MOTION:** Teacher holds right palm to show word. Add the final sound with left hand and lightly clap hands together for the whole word.

**LESSON FOCUS:** When we hear whole words, we can take a sound away and say what is left. Sometimes taking away a sound makes a new word, and other times, it is just a word part that is left.

⊕ Lesson 15: Deleting Final Phonemes

Teacher Directions: I will say a word. You will say the word back to me. We will take away or delete the final sound and you will tell me what is left.

Student Response: Students repeat the word aloud, then say the new word without the final phoneme.

| WHOLE WORD: | WITHOUT | WHAT'S LEFT IS: |
|------|------|------|
| paste | /t/ | pace |
| scorch | /ch/ | score |
| handle | /l/ | hand |

| WHOLE WORD: | WITHOUT | WHAT'S LEFT IS: |
|------|------|------|
| wĭnd | /d/ | win |
| perk | /k/ | per |
| drawn | /n/ | draw |

✋ **DELETING HAND MOTION:** Hold 2 palms out in front of you. Teacher's left hand is the final sound, right hand is the rest of the word. Pull left hand away when deleting the final phoneme, and show what part remains with your right hand.

**TEACHER TIP:**

/*/ Always add or delete the sound, not the letter name

# Adding & Deleting Final Phonemes

**LESSON FOCUS:** When we say a word or a word part, we can add a sound at the end to make a new word.

⇨ Lesson 16: Adding Final Phonemes

Teacher Directions: I will say a word. You will say it back to me. We will add a sound at the end and you will tell me the new word.

Student Response: Students repeat the first word aloud, then say the new word with the final phoneme the teacher provided.

| SAY: | ADD /*/ AT THE END | THE WORD IS: |
|------|--------------------|--------------|
| pain | /t/ | paint |
| were | /k/ | work |
| class | /p/ | clasp |

| SAY: | ADD /*/ AT THE END | THE WORD IS: |
|------|--------------------|--------------|
| pow | /ch/ | pouch |
| store | /m/ | storm |
| cloud | /ē/ | cloudy |

🖐 **ADDING HAND MOTION:** Teacher holds right palm to show word. Add the final sound with left hand and lightly clap hands together for the whole word.

**LESSON FOCUS:** When we hear whole words, we can take a sound away and say what is left. Sometimes taking away a sound makes a new word, and other times, it is just a word part that is left.

⇨ Lesson 16: Deleting Final Phonemes

Teacher Directions: I will say a word. You will say the word back to me. We will take away or delete the final sound and you will tell me what is left.

Student Response: Students repeat the word aloud, then say the new word without the final phoneme.

| WHOLE WORD: | WITHOUT | WHAT'S LEFT IS: |
|-------------|---------|-----------------|
| belt | /t/ | bell |
| wild | /d/ | while |
| news | /z/ | new |

| WHOLE WORD: | WITHOUT | WHAT'S LEFT IS: |
|-------------|---------|-----------------|
| went | /t/ | when |
| burn | /n/ | burr |
| couch | /ch/ | cow |

🖐 **DELETING HAND MOTION:** Hold 2 palms out in front of you. Teacher's left hand is the final sound, right hand is the rest of the word. Pull left hand away when deleting the final phoneme, and show what part remains with your right hand.

---

**TEACHER TIP:**

/*/ Always add or delete the sound, not the letter name

# Adding & Deleting Final Phonemes

**LESSON FOCUS:** When we say a word or a word part, we can add a sound at the end to make a new word.

⟳ Lesson 17: Adding Final Phonemes

Teacher Directions: I will say a word or word part. You will say it back to me. We will add a sound at the end and you will tell me the new word.

Student Response: Students repeat the first word aloud, then say the new word with the final phoneme the teacher provided.

| SAY: | ADD /*/ AT THE END | THE WORD IS: |
|---|---|---|
| mass | /t/ | mast |
| fine | /d/ | find |
| limb | /p/ | limp |

| SAY: | ADD /*/ AT THE END | THE WORD IS: |
|---|---|---|
| bran | /ch/ | branch |
| prin | /t/ | print |
| shell | /f/ | shelf |

✋ **ADDING HAND MOTION:** Teacher holds right palm to show word. Add the final sound with left hand and lightly clap hands together for the whole word.

**LESSON FOCUS:** When we hear whole words, we can take a sound away and say what is left. Sometimes taking away a sound makes a new word, and other times, it is just a word part that is left.

⟳ Lesson 17: Deleting Final Phonemes

Teacher Directions: I will say a word. You will say the word back to me. We will take away or delete the final sound and you will tell me what is left.

Student Response: Students repeat the word aloud, then say the new word without the final phoneme.

| WHOLE WORD: | WITHOUT | WHAT'S LEFT IS: |
|---|---|---|
| mist | /t/ | miss |
| mask | /k/ | mass |
| wealth | /th/ | well |

| WHOLE WORD: | WITHOUT | WHAT'S LEFT IS: |
|---|---|---|
| thump | /p/ | thumb |
| bunch | /ch/ | bun |
| hoop | /p/ | who |

✋ **DELETING HAND MOTION:** Hold 2 palms out in front of you. Teacher's left hand is the final sound, right hand is the rest of the word. Pull left hand away when deleting the final phoneme, and show what part remains with your right hand.

🍎

**TEACHER TIP:**

/*/ Always add or delete the sound, not the letter name

# Adding & Deleting Final Phonemes

**LESSON FOCUS:** When we say a word or a word part, we can add a sound at the end to make a new word.

⇨ Lesson 18: Adding Final Phonemes

Teacher Directions: I will say a word/word part. You will say it back to me. We will add a sound at the end and you will tell me the new word.

Student Response: Students repeat the first word aloud, then say the new word with the final phoneme the teacher provided.

| SAY: | ADD /*/ AT THE END | THE WORD IS: | SAY: | ADD /*/ AT THE END | THE WORD IS: |
|------|--------------------|--------------|------|--------------------|--------------|
| class | /p/ | clasp | pro | /z/ | pros |
| pin | /ch/ | pinch | lun | /ch/ | lunch |
| lass | /t/ | last | men | /t/ | meant |

✋ **ADDING HAND MOTION:** Teacher holds right palm to show word. Add the final sound with left hand and lightly clap hands together for the whole word.

**LESSON FOCUS:** When we hear whole words, we can take a sound away and say what is left. Sometimes taking away a sound makes a new word, and other times, it is just a word part that is left.

⇨ Lesson 18: Deleting Final Phonemes

Teacher Directions: I will say a word. You will say the word back to me. We will take away or delete the final sound and you will tell me what is left.

Student Response: Students repeat the word aloud, then say the new word without the final phoneme.

| WHOLE WORD: | WITHOUT | WHAT'S LEFT IS: | WHOLE WORD: | WITHOUT | WHAT'S LEFT IS: |
|-------------|---------|-----------------|-------------|---------|-----------------|
| dent | /t/ | den | change | /j/ | chain |
| ranch | /ch/ | ran | quilt | /t/ | quill |
| fourth | /th/ | four | punch | /ch/ | pun |

✋ **DELETING HAND MOTION:** Hold 2 palms out in front of you. Teacher's left hand is the final sound, right hand is the rest of the word. Pull left hand away when deleting the final phoneme, and show what part remains with your right hand.

🍎

**TEACHER TIP:**

/*/ Always add or delete the sound, not the letter name

# Adding & Deleting Final Phonemes

**LESSON FOCUS:** When we say a word or a word part, we can add a sound at the end to make a new word.

⇨ Lesson 19: Adding Final Phonemes

Teacher Directions: I will say a word/word part. You will say it back to me. We will add a sound at the end and you will tell me the new word.

Student Response: Students repeat the first word aloud, then say the new word with the final phoneme the teacher provided.

| SAY: | ADD /*/ AT THE END | THE WORD IS: |
|------|------|------|
| score | /ch/ | scorch |
| lease | /t/ | least |
| mole | /d/ | mold |

| SAY: | ADD /*/ AT THE END | THE WORD IS: |
|------|------|------|
| plea | /z/ | please |
| true | /p/ | troop |
| fray | /m/ | frame |

✋ ADDING HAND MOTION: Teacher holds right palm to show word. Add the final sound with left hand and lightly clap hands together for the whole word.

**LESSON FOCUS:** When we hear whole words, we can take a sound away and say what is left. Sometimes taking away a sound makes a new word, and other times, it is just a word part that is left.

⇨ Lesson 19: Deleting Final Phonemes

Teacher Directions: I will say a word. You will say the word back to me. We will take away or delete the final sound and you will tell me what is left.

Student Response: Students repeat the word aloud, then say the new word without the final phoneme.

| WHOLE WORD: | WITHOUT | WHAT'S LEFT IS: |
|------|------|------|
| bust | /t/ | bus |
| tend | /d/ | ten |
| pant | /t/ | pan |

| WHOLE WORD: | WITHOUT | WHAT'S LEFT IS: |
|------|------|------|
| stern | /n/ | stir |
| wild | /d/ | while |
| north | /th/ | nor |

✋ DELETING HAND MOTION: Hold 2 palms out in front of you. Teacher's left hand is the final sound, right hand is the rest of the word. Pull left hand away when deleting the final phoneme, and show what part remains with your right hand.

**TEACHER TIP:**

/*/ Always add or delete the sound, not the letter name

# Adding & Deleting Final Phonemes

**LESSON FOCUS:** When we say a word or a word part, we can add a sound at the end to make a new word.

## Lesson 20: Adding Final Phonemes

Teacher Directions: I will say a word/word part. You will say it back to me. We will add a sound at the end and you will tell me the new word.

Student Response: Students repeat the first word or word part aloud, then say the new word with the final phoneme the teacher provided.

| SAY: | ADD /*/ AT THE END | THE WORD IS: |
|------|--------------------|--------------|
| car | /p/ | carp |
| store | /m/ | storm |
| tie | /d/ | tide |

| SAY: | ADD /*/ AT THE END | THE WORD IS: |
|------|--------------------|--------------|
| flew | /t/ | flute |
| snee | /k/ | sneak |
| four | /th/ | fourth |

✋ **ADDING HAND MOTION:** Teacher holds right palm to show word. Add the final sound with left hand and lightly clap hands together for the whole word.

**LESSON FOCUS:** When we hear whole words, we can take a sound away and say what is left. Sometimes taking away a sound makes a new word, and other times, it is just a word part that is left.

## Lesson 20: Deleting Final Phonemes

Teacher Directions: I will say a word. You will say the word back to me. We will take away or delete the final sound and you will tell me what is left.

Student Response: Students repeat the word aloud, then say the new word without the final phoneme.

| WHOLE WORD: | WITHOUT | WHAT'S LEFT IS: |
|-------------|---------|-----------------|
| bald | /d/ | ball |
| wrench | /ch/ | wren |
| yelp | /p/ | yell |

| WHOLE WORD: | WITHOUT | WHAT'S LEFT IS: |
|-------------|---------|-----------------|
| stove | /v/ | stōw |
| graft | /t/ | graph |
| launch | /ch/ | lawn |

✋ **DELETING HAND MOTION:** Hold 2 palms out in front of you. Teacher's left hand is the final sound, right hand is the rest of the word. Pull left hand away when deleting the final phoneme, and show what part remains with your right hand.

**TEACHER TIP:**

/*/ Always add or delete the sound, not the letter name

# Adding Final Phonemes

We have worked on many lessons with adding a sound to a word or word part to make a new word. Today, you are going to show me what you have learned.

Teacher Administration Directions: I will say a word or word part. You will say it back to me. I will tell you a sound to add at the end, and you will tell me the new word.

Recording Directions: Record incorrect responses in the Student Response column. If correct, mark with a check or +

Student Name: _____     Date: _____

|  | WORD: | ADD /*/ AT THE END: | CORRECT RESPONSE: | STUDENT RESPONSE: |
|---|---|---|---|---|
| 1 | plan | /t/ | plant | |
| 2 | stow | /v/ | stove | |
| 3 | paw | /n/ | pawn | |
| 4 | ram | /p/ | ramp | |
| 5 | brow | /n/ | brown | |
| 6 | how | /s/ | house | |
| 7 | who | /p/ | hoop | |
| 8 | away | /k/ | awake | |
| 9 | thumb | /p/ | thump | |
| 10 | voy | /s/ | voice | |
| | | | | Score:     /10 |

**SCORING GUIDE:**

0-5 correct:  Review Adding Final Phonemes Lessons 11-20

6-8 correct:  Review Adding Final Phonemes Lessons 16-20

9-10 correct:  Move on to Adding Phonemes with Consonant Blends, Lessons 21-23

# Deleting Final Phonemes

We have worked on many lessons with deleting a sound in a word to say what is left. Today, you are going to show me what you have learned.

Teacher Administration Directions: I will say a word. You will say it back to me. I will tell you a sound to delete or take away from the end. You will tell me what is left.

Recording Directions: Record incorrect responses in the Student Response column. If correct, mark with a check or +

Student Name: _____     Date: _____

|   | WORD: | WITHOUT /*/ | CORRECT RESPONSE: | STUDENT RESPONSE: |
|---|-------|-------------|-------------------|-------------------|
| 1 | torch | /ch/ | tore | |
| 2 | handle | /l/ | hand | |
| 3 | place | /s/ | play | |
| 4 | tooth | /th/ | too | |
| 5 | croak | /k/ | crow | |
| 6 | wave | /v/ | way | |
| 7 | perch | /ch/ | per | |
| 8 | court | /t/ | core | |
| 9 | claws | /z/ | claw | |
| 10 | treat | /t/ | tree | |

Score:     /10

SCORING GUIDE:

0-5 correct:  Review Deleting Final Phonemes Lessons 11-20

6-8 correct:  Review Deleting Final Phonemes Lessons 16-20

9-10 correct:  Move on to Deleting Phonemes with Consonant Blends, Lessons 21-23

# Adding & Deleting Phonemes with Blends

**LESSON FOCUS:** We can make a new word by adding a second sound to a word or word part. In these lessons, we will add a second sound to create a consonant blend.

⇨ Lesson 21: Adding a 2nd Sound to Make a Consonant Blend

Teacher Directions: I will say a word.  You will say it back to me. We will add a 2nd sound to create a blend. I will say, "Add /*/ after /*/," and you will tell me the new word.

Example:  Say bow. Add /l/ after /b/ and the word is?  Blow

Student Response: Students repeat the whole word and say the new word with the consonant blend.

| SAY: | ADD /*/ AFTER /*/ | THE WORD IS: |
|------|-------------------|--------------|
| go | /l/ after /g/ | glow |
| sap | /n/ after /s/ | snap |
| say | /w/ after /s/ | sway |

| SAY: | ADD /*/ AFTER /*/ | THE WORD IS: |
|------|-------------------|--------------|
| cash | /r/ after /c/ | crash |
| sigh | /p/ after /s/ | spy |
| few | /l/ after /f/ | flew |

**TEACHER TIPS:**
1. Segment the word into phonemes and then add the new sound: go, /g-o/. When I add /l/, the sounds are /g-l-ō/, glow
2. /*/ Say sound, not letter name

**LESSON FOCUS:** When we hear whole words, we can take a sound away and say what is left. In these lessons, we will delete or take away the second sound from a consonant blend.

⇨ Lesson 21: Deleting the 2nd Sound from a Consonant Blend

Teacher Directions: I will say a word. You will say the word back to me. We will take away or delete the 2nd sound from the beginning blend and you will tell me the new word.

Example:  Say slow.  Without /l/, the word is so.

Student Response:  Students repeat the word aloud, then say the new word without the 2nd sound of the consonant blend.

| WHOLE WORD: | WITHOUT | WHAT'S LEFT IS: |
|-------------|---------|-----------------|
| blow | /l/ | bōw |
| free | /r/ | fee |
| store | /t/ | sore |

| WHOLE WORD: | WITHOUT | WHAT'S LEFT IS: |
|-------------|---------|-----------------|
| spoon | /p/ | soon |
| bright | /r/ | bite |
| stick | /t/ | sick |

**TEACHER TIPS:**
1. Segment the word into phonemes and then delete the new sound. The word blow has 3 sounds: /b-l-ow/. When we delete /l/, what's left is b-ow, bow.
2. /*/ Say sound, not letter name

# Adding & Deleting Phonemes with Blends

**LESSON FOCUS:** We can make a new word by adding a second sound to a word or word part. In these lessons, we will add a second sound to create a consonant blend.

⇨ Lesson 22: Adding a 2nd Sound to Make a Consonant Blend

Teacher Directions: I will say a word. You will say it back to me. We will add a 2nd sound to create a blend. I will say, "Add /*/ after /*/," and you will tell me the new word.

Student Response: Students repeat the whole word and say the new word with the consonant blend.

| SAY: | ADD /*/ AFTER /*/ | THE WORD IS: |
|------|-------------------|--------------|
| sight | Add /l/ after /s/ | slight |
| book | Add /r/ after /b/ | brook |
| sale | Add /c/ after /s/ | scale |

| SAY: | ADD /*/ AFTER /*/ | THE WORD IS: |
|------|-------------------|--------------|
| gate | Add /r/ after /g/ | grate/great |
| see | Add /k/ after /s/ | ski |
| side | Add /p/ after /s/ | spied |

**TEACHER TIPS:**
1. Segment the word into phonemes and then add the new sound: go, /g-o/. When I add /l/, the sounds are /g-l-ō/, glow
2. /*/ Say sound, not letter name

**LESSON FOCUS:** When we hear whole words, we can take a sound away and say what is left. In these lessons, we will delete or take away the second sound from a consonant blend.

⇨ Lesson 22: Deleting the 2nd Sound from a Consonant Blend

Teacher Directions: I will say a word. You will say the word back to me. We will take away or delete the 2nd sound from the beginning blend and you will tell me the new word.

Student Response: Students repeat the word aloud, then say the new word without the 2nd sound of the consonant blend.

| WHOLE WORD: | WITHOUT | WHAT'S LEFT IS: |
|-------------|---------|-----------------|
| slope | /l/ | soap |
| frame | /r/ | fame |
| steam | /t/ | seem |

| WHOLE WORD: | WITHOUT | WHAT'S LEFT IS: |
|-------------|---------|-----------------|
| crave | /r/ | cave |
| snake | /n/ | sake |
| plant | /l/ | pant |

**TEACHER TIP:** If students struggle to add or delete the second sound, use felt or counters to represent the sounds.

For adding, show a rectangle and the square to represent the initial sound and rime; insert a second rectangle when adding the second sound of the blend.

For deleting, show two rectangles to represent the two sounds of the blend and the square to represent the rime. Pull the second rectangle away when deleting the second sound.

# Adding & Deleting Phonemes with Blends

**LESSON FOCUS:** We can make a new word by adding a second sound to a word or word part. In these lessons, we will add a second sound to create a consonant blend.

⊕ Lesson 23: Adding a 2nd Sound to Make a Consonant Blend

Teacher Directions: I will say a word.  You will say it back to me. We will add a 2nd sound to create a blend. I will say, "Add /*/ after /*/," and you will tell me the new word.

Student Response: Students repeat the whole word and say the new word with the consonant blend.

| SAY: | ADD /*/ AFTER /*/ | THE WORD IS: |
|------|-------------------|--------------|
| fake | /l/ after /f/ | flake |
| camp | /r/ after /k/ | cramp |
| sign | /w/ after /s/ | swine |

| SAY: | ADD /*/ AFTER /*/ | THE WORD IS: |
|------|-------------------|--------------|
| sell | /p/ after /s/ | spell |
| gaze | /r/ after /g/ | graze |
| four | /l/ after /f/ | floor |

🍎 TEACHER TIP: Segment the word into phonemes and then add the new sound: go, /g-o/. When I add /l/, the sounds are /g-l-ō/, glow

**LESSON FOCUS:** When we hear whole words, we can take a sound away and say what is left. In these lessons, we will delete or take away the second sound from a consonant blend.

⊕ Lesson 23: Deleting the 2nd Sound from a Consonant Blend

Teacher Directions: I will say a word. You will say the word back to me. We will take away or delete the 2nd sound from the beginning blend and you will tell me the new word.

Student Response:  Students repeat the word aloud, then say the new word without the 2nd sound of the consonant blend.

| WHOLE WORD: | WITHOUT | WHAT'S LEFT IS: |
|-------------|---------|-----------------|
| frog | /r/ | fog |
| sweet | /w/ | seat |
| grain | /r/ | gain |

| WHOLE WORD: | WITHOUT | WHAT'S LEFT IS: |
|-------------|---------|-----------------|
| bleed | /l/ | bead |
| sneeze | /n/ | seize |
| plot | /l/ | pot |

🍎 TEACHER TIP:  If students struggle to add or delete the second sound, use felt or counters to represent the sounds.

For adding, show a rectangle and the square to represent the initial sound and rime; insert a second rectangle when adding the second sound of the blend.

For deleting, show two rectangles to represent the two sounds of the blend and the square to represent the rime.  Pull the second rectangle away when deleting the second sound.

# Adding Phonemes: Beginning Blends

We have worked on many lessons with adding a sound to a word or word part to make a new word. Today, you are going to show me what you have learned.

Teacher Administration Directions: I will say a word. You will say it back to me. I will tell you the sound to add to create a consonant blend, and you will tell me the new word.

Recording Directions: Record incorrect responses in the Student Response column. If correct, mark with a check or +

Student Name: _____     Date: _____

|   | WORD: | ADD /*/ AFTER /*/ | CORRECT RESPONSE: | STUDENT RESPONSE: |
|---|-------|-------------------|-------------------|-------------------|
| 1 | boom | Add /r/ after /b/ | broom | |
| 2 | sail | Add /n/ after /s/ | snail | |
| 3 | fame | Add /l/ after /f/ | flame | |
| 4 | gate | Add /r/ after /g/ | great | |
| 5 | side | Add /p/ after /s/ | spied | |
| 6 | sake | Add /t/ after /s/ | steak | |
| | | | | Score:      /6 |

SCORING GUIDE:

0-4 correct: Review Adding Phonemes with Consonant Blends, Lessons 21-23

5-6 correct: Move on to Adding Ending Blends 24-26

# Deleting Phonemes: Beginning Blends

We have worked on many lessons with deleting a sound from a word to to say what is left. Today, you are going to show me what you have learned.

Teacher Administration Directions: I will say a word. You will say it back to me. I will tell you the 2nd sound of the blend to delete or take away. You will tell me what is left.

Recording Directions: Record incorrect responses in the Student Response column. If correct, mark with a check or +

Student Name: _____       Date: _____

| | WORD: | WITHOUT /*/ | CORRECT RESPONSE: | STUDENT RESPONSE: |
|---|---|---|---|---|
| 1 | praise | /r/ | pays | |
| 2 | spoke | /p/ | soak | |
| 3 | ski | /k/ | see | |
| 4 | stay | /t/ | say | |
| 5 | free | /r/ | fee | |
| 6 | bleed | /l/ | bead | |
| | | | | Score:        /6 |

SCORING GUIDE:

0-4 correct: Review Deleting Phonemes from a Blend Lessons 21-23

5-6 correct: Move on to Mixed Review Lessons 24-26

# Adding & Deleting with Ending Blends

**LESSON FOCUS:** We have been adding a sound to make a consonant blend at the beginning of words. Now we will add a sound to make a blend at the end of a word.

⇨ Lesson 24: Adding a Phoneme to Make an Ending Blend

Teacher Directions: I will say a word. You will say it back to me. We will add a sound to create a blend at the end of the word. I will say, "Add /*/ after /*/," and the you will tell me the new word.

Student Response: Students repeat the whole word and say the new word with the consonant blend.

| SAY: | ADD /*/ AFTER /*/ | THE WORD IS: |
|------|-------------------|--------------|
| tote | Add /s/ after /ō/ | toast |
| pet  | Add /s/ after /ĕ/ | pest |
| cap  | Add /m/ after /ă/ | camp |

| SAY: | ADD /*/ AFTER /*/ | THE WORD IS: |
|------|-------------------|--------------|
| jet  | Add /s/ after /ĕ/ | jest |
| gap  | Add /s/ after /ă/ | gasp |
| rat  | Add /f/ after /ă/ | raft |

🍎 **TEACHER TIP:** Segment the word into phonemes and then add the new sound: tote, /t-ō-t/. When I add /s/ after /ō/, I hear 4 sounds, /t-ō-s-t/, toast.

**LESSON FOCUS:** We have been deleting a sound from a blend at the beginning of a word. Now we will delete or take away a sound from a blend at the end of a word.

⇨ Lesson 24: Deleting a Phoneme from an Ending Consonant Blend

Teacher Directions: I will say a word. You will say the word back to me. We will take away or delete a sound from the ending blend and you will tell me the new word.

Student Response: Students repeat the word aloud, then say the new word without the sound of the consonant blend.

| WHOLE WORD: | WITHOUT | WHAT'S LEFT IS: |
|-------------|---------|-----------------|
| best   | /s/ | bet |
| lift   | /f/ | lit |
| kissed | /s/ | kit |

| WHOLE WORD: | WITHOUT | WHAT'S LEFT IS: |
|-------------|---------|-----------------|
| task | /s/ | tack |
| wept | /p/ | wet |
| past | /s/ | pat |

🍎

**TEACHER TIPS:**

① /*/ Add and Delete the sound, not the letter name

② Segment the word into phonemes and then say the phonemes without the deleted sound. Example: The word is best, /b-e-s-t/. Without /s/, the sounds are /b-e-t/, bet.

# Adding & Deleting with Ending Blends

LESSON FOCUS: We will add a sound to make a consonant blend at the end of a word.

⇨ Lesson 25: Adding a Phoneme to Make an Ending Blend

Teacher Directions: I will say a word. You will say it back to me. We will add a sound to create a blend at the end of the word. I will say, "Add /*/ after /*/," and the you will tell me the new word.

Student Response: Students repeat the whole word and say the new word with the consonant blend.

| SAY: | ADD /*/ AFTER /*/ | THE WORD IS: |
|------|-------------------|--------------|
| net | Add /s/ after /ĕ/ | nest |
| lap | Add /m/ after /ă/ | lamp |
| code | Add /l/ after /ō/ | cold |

| SAY: | ADD /*/ AFTER /*/ | THE WORD IS: |
|------|-------------------|--------------|
| sit | Add /f/ after /ĭ/ | sift |
| rote | Add /s/ after /ō/ | roast |
| mit | Add /s/ after /ĭ/ | mist |

**TEACHER TIP:** Segment the word into phonemes and then add the new sound: net, /n-e-t/. When I add /s/ after /ĕ/, I hear 4 sounds: /n-e-s-t/, nest

LESSON FOCUS: We will delete or take away a sound from a blend at the end of a word.

⇨ Lesson 25: Deleting a Phoneme from an Ending Consonant Blend

Teacher Directions: I will say a word. You will say the word back to me. We will take away or delete a sound from the ending blend and you will tell me the new word.

Student Response: Students repeat the word aloud, then say the new word without the sound of the consonant blend.

| WHOLE WORD: | WITHOUT | WHAT'S LEFT IS: |
|-------------|---------|-----------------|
| list | /s/ | lit |
| chomp | /m/ | chop |
| left | /f/ | let |

| WHOLE WORD: | WITHOUT | WHAT'S LEFT IS: |
|-------------|---------|-----------------|
| desk | /s/ | deck |
| brisk | /s/ | brick |
| slipped | /p/ | slit |

**TEACHER TIPS:**

① /*/ Add and Delete the sound, not the letter name

② Segment the word into phonemes and then say the phonemes without the deleted sound. Example: The word is best, /b-e-s-t/. Without /s/, the sounds are /b-e-t/, bet.

# Adding & Deleting with Ending Blends

**LESSON FOCUS:** We will add a sound to make a consonant blend at the end of a word.

⇨ Lesson 26: Adding a Phoneme to Make an Ending Blend

Teacher Directions: I will say a word. You will say it back to me. We will add a sound to create a blend at the end of the word. I will say, "Add /*/ after /*/," and the you will tell me the new word.

Student Response: Students repeat the whole word and say the new word with the consonant blend.

| SAY: | ADD /*/ AFTER /*/ | THE WORD IS: |
|------|-------------------|--------------|
| boat | Add /s/ after /ō/ | boast |
| stop | Add /m/ after /ŏ/ | stomp |
| duck | Add /s/ after /ŭ/ | dusk |

| SAY: | ADD /*/ AFTER /*/ | THE WORD IS: |
|------|-------------------|--------------|
| eat | Add /s/ after / ē/ | east |
| coat | Add /l/ after /ō/ | colt |
| mutt | Add /s/ after /ŭ/ | must |

🍎 **TEACHER TIP:** Segment the word into phonemes and then add the new sound: boat, /b-ō-t/, When I add /s/ after /ō/, I hear 4 sounds: /b-ō-s-t/, boast

**LESSON FOCUS:** We will delete or take away a sound from a blend at the end of a word.

⇨ Lesson 26: Deleting a Phoneme from an Ending Consonant Blend

Teacher Directions: I will say a word. You will say the word back to me. We will take away or delete a sound from the ending blend and you will tell me the new word.

Student Response: Students repeat the word aloud, then say the new word without the sound of the consonant blend.

| WHOLE WORD: | WITHOUT | WHAT'S LEFT IS: |
|-------------|---------|-----------------|
| guest | /s/ | get |
| bolt | /l/ | boat |
| rust | /s/ | rut |

| WHOLE WORD: | WITHOUT | WHAT'S LEFT IS: |
|-------------|---------|-----------------|
| east | /s/ | eat |
| chimp | /m/ | chip |
| west | /s/ | wet |

🍎

**TEACHER TIPS:**

① /*/ Add and Delete the sound, not the letter name

② Segment the word into phonemes and then say the phonemes without the deleted sound. Example: The word is best, /b-e-s-t/. Without /s/, the sounds are /b-e-t/, bet.

# Adding Phonemes: Ending Blends

We have worked on many lessons with adding a sound to a word or word part to make a new word. Today, you will show me what you have learned.

Teacher Administration Directions: I will say a word. You will say it back to me. I will tell you a sound to add to create an ending blend.  You will tell me the new word.

Recording Directions: Record incorrect responses in the Student Response column. If correct, mark with a check or +

Student Name: _____     Date: _____

|   | WORD: | ADD /*/ AFTER /*/ | CORRECT RESPONSE: | STUDENT RESPONSE: |
|---|-------|-------------------|-------------------|-------------------|
| 1 | lap   | Add /m/ after /ă/ | lamp  |  |
| 2 | lit   | Add /s/ after /ĭ/ | list  |  |
| 3 | net   | Add /s/ after /ĕ/ | nest  |  |
| 4 | sit   | Add /f/ after /ĭ/ | sift  |  |
| 5 | chop  | Add /m/ after /ŏ/ | chomp |  |
| 6 | duck  | Add /s/ after /ŭ/ | dusk  |  |
| | | | | Score:      /6 |

## SCORING GUIDE:

0-4 correct: Review Adding Ending Blends 24-26

5-6 correct: Move on to Mixed Review 27-28

# Deleting Phonemes: Ending Blends

We have worked on many lessons with deleting a sound from a word to make a new word or say what is left. Today, you will show me what you have learned.

Teacher Administration Directions: I will say a word. I will tell you a sound to delete or take away from the ending blend. You will tell me the new word.

Recording Directions: Record incorrect responses in the Student Response column. If correct, mark with a check or +

Student Name: _____     Date: _____

|  | WORD: | WITHOUT /*/ | CORRECT RESPONSE: | STUDENT RESPONSE: |
|---|---|---|---|---|
| 1 | toast | /s/ | tote | |
| 2 | left | /f/ | let | |
| 3 | fast | /s/ | fat | |
| 4 | pact | /k/ | pat | |
| 5 | mist | /s/ | mitt | |
| 6 | lisp | /s/ | lip | |
| | | | | Score:      /6 |

SCORING GUIDE:

0-4 correct: Review Deleting Ending Blends 24-26

5-6 correct: Move on to Mixed Review 27-28

# Adding & Deleting Phonemes: Mixed Review

LESSON FOCUS: We have practiced adding and deleting sounds from the beginning and end of words. We will be reviewing these skills by adding and deleting a sound from different places in a word.

⇨ Lesson 27: Adding Phonemes to a Word

Teacher Directions: I will say a word.  You will say it back to me.  We will add a sound to create a new word. Listen carefully for where the sound is being added to the word.

Student Response: Students repeat the whole word and say the new word with the added sound.

| SAY: | ADD: | THE WORD IS: |
|------|------|--------------|
| lizard | /b/ at the beginning | blizzard |
| fog | /r/ after /f/ | frog |
| lit | /s/ after /ĭ/ | list |

| SAY: | ADD: | THE WORD IS: |
|------|------|--------------|
| were | /k/ at the end | work |
| moat | /s/ after /ō/ | most |
| fame | /l/ after /f/ | flame |

**TEACHER TIP:**
When completing this lesson you will need to note where the student is adding the sound to the word. You will provide the student with the instructions to add before or after a sound.

⇨ Lesson 27: Deleting Phonemes from a Word

Teacher Directions: I will say a word. You will say the word back to me. We will take away or delete a sound from different places in a word. You will tell me what is left.

Student Response: Students repeat the whole word aloud, take the sound away and say the new word.

| WHOLE WORD: | WITHOUT | WHAT'S LEFT IS: |
|-------------|---------|-----------------|
| stale | /l/ | stay |
| brand | /r/ | band |
| swept | /p/ | sweat |

| WHOLE WORD: | WITHOUT | WHAT'S LEFT IS: |
|-------------|---------|-----------------|
| stock | /s/ | tock |
| mast | /s/ | mat |
| flush | /f/ | lush |

**TEACHER TIP:**
/*/ Add and Delete the sound, not the letter name

# Adding & Deleting Phonemes: Mixed Review

LESSON FOCUS: We have practiced adding and deleting sounds from the beginning and end of words. We will be reviewing these skills by adding and deleting a sound from different places in the word.

⇨ Lesson 28: Adding Phonemes to a Word

Teacher Directions: I will say a word. You will say it back to me. We will add a sound to make a new word.

Student Response: Students repeat the whole word and say the new word with the added sound.

| SAY: | ADD: | THE WORD IS: |
|---|---|---|
| teaser | /w/ after /t/ | tweezer |
| layer | /p/ at the beginning | player |
| blue | /m/ at the end | bloom |

| SAY: | ADD: | THE WORD IS: |
|---|---|---|
| sad | /n/ after /ă/ | sand |
| gate | /r/ after /g/ | great |
| red | /th/ at the beginning | thread |

**TEACHER TIPS:**
When completing this lesson you will need to note where the student is adding the sound to the word. You will provide the student with the instructions to add before or after a sound.

⇨ Lesson 28: Deleting Phonemes from a Word

Teacher Directions: I will say a word. You will say the word back to me. We will take away or delete a sound from different places in a word. You will tell me what is left.

Student Response: Students repeat the whole word aloud, take the sound away and say the new word.

| WHOLE WORD: | WITHOUT | WHAT'S LEFT IS: |
|---|---|---|
| praise | /p/ | raise |
| surf | /f/ | sir |
| snake | /n/ | sake |

| WHOLE WORD: | WITHOUT | WHAT'S LEFT IS: |
|---|---|---|
| thrush | /th/ | rush |
| wonder | /w/ | under |
| past | /s/ | pat |

**TEACHER TIP:**
/*/ Add and Delete the sound, not the letter name

# Anchor Lesson: Substituting Initial Phonemes

LESSON FOCUS: When we substitute the initial phoneme, we change the first or initial sound in a word to make a new word. In these lessons, I will say a word and we will substitute the first sound to make a new word.

## I DO:

I will show you how I can make a new word by changing or substituting the first sound in a word.

| night | T: The word is bite. When I change /b/ to /n/, the word is /n-ight/, night. |
| bark | T: The word is park. When I change /p/ to /b/, the word is /b-ark/, bark. |

## WE DO:

Let's try some words together. I will say the word. You will repeat the word. We will substitute the first sound and say the new word.

| hot | T: Say, got |
|     | T & S: got |
|     | T: Change /g/ to /h/ and the word is? |
|     | T & S: hot |
| shown | T: Say, loan |
|       | T & S: loan |
|       | T: Change /l/ to /sh/ and word is? |
|       | T & S: shown |

## YOU DO:

I will say a word. You will repeat the word. I will tell you the sound to substitute at the beginning, and you will tell me the new word.

| SAY: | CHANGE /*/ TO /*/ | THE WORD IS: |
|------|-------------------|--------------|
| meet | /m/ to /s/ | seat |
| rip | /r/ to /z/ | zip |
| hook | /h/ to /b/ | book |

✋ **SUBSTITUTING HAND MOTION:**

Teacher holds 2 closed fists, touching at the thumbs, out in front to show the whole word. Right fist is the first sound, left fist is the rest of the word. Pull the right fist away when changing the first sound and lightly pound your fists together when you say the new word.

🍎

**TEACHER TIPS:**

① If students struggle to change the intial sound, use felt or counters to represent the word:
 ██ ██ Pull the first rectangle away when changing the sound and replace it when saying the new word.

② /*/ Substitute the sound, not the letter name

# Substituting Initial Phonemes

LESSON FOCUS: When we substitute the initial phoneme, we change the first or initial sound to make a new word. In these lessons, I will say a word and we will substitute the first sound to make a new word.

Teacher Directions: I will say a word. You will repeat the word. We will substitute the first sound and you will tell me the new word.

Student Response: Students repeat the first word aloud, change the intial sound, and say the new word.

⇨ Lesson 29

| SAY: | CHANGE /*/ TO /*/ | THE WORD IS: |
|------|-------------------|--------------|
| like | /l/ to /b/ | bike |
| cope | /k/ to /s/ | soap |
| race | /r/ to /f/ | face |
| mail | /m/ to /p/ | pail |
| tire | /t/ to /f/ | fire |
| night | /n/ to /k/ | kite |

⇨ Lesson 30

| SAY: | CHANGE /*/ TO /*/ | THE WORD IS: |
|------|-------------------|--------------|
| part | /p/ to /h/ | heart |
| teach | /t/ to /b/ | beach |
| rain | /r/ to /ch/ | chain |
| woke | /w/ to /y/ | yoke |
| base | /b/ to /v/ | vase |
| peak | /p/ to /w/ | weak |

SUBSTITUTING HAND MOTION: Teacher holds 2 closed fists, touching at the thumbs, out in front to show the whole word. Right fist is the first sound, left fist is the rest of the word. Pull the right fist away when changing the first sound and lightly pound your fists together when you say the new word.

## TEACHER TIPS:

① If students struggle to change the intial sound, use felt or counters to represent the word:
   ■ ■ Pull the first rectangle away when changing the sound and replace it when saying the new word.

② /*/ Substitute the sound, not the letter name

# Substituting Initial Phonemes

LESSON FOCUS: When we substitute the initial phoneme, we change the first or initial sound to make a new word. In these lessons, I will say a word and we will substitute the first sound to make a new word.

Teacher Directions: I will say a word. You will repeat the word. We will substitute the first sound and you will tell me the new word.

Student Response: Students repeat the first word aloud, change the intial sound, and say the new word.

### ⇨ Lesson 31

| SAY: | CHANGE /*/ TO /*/ | THE WORD IS: |
|------|-------------------|--------------|
| many | /m/ to /p/ | penny |
| better | /b/ to /l/ | letter |
| table | /t/ to /f/ | fable |
| custard | /c/ to /m/ | mustard |
| soaring | /s/ to /r/ | roaring |
| pillow | /p/ to /w/ | willow |

### ⇨ Lesson 32

| SAY: | CHANGE /*/ TO /*/ | THE WORD IS: |
|------|-------------------|--------------|
| sheet | /sh/ to /wh/ | wheat |
| seek | /s/ to /ch/ | cheek |
| that | /th/ to /r/ | rat |
| shown | /sh/ to /b/ | bone |
| dance | /d/ to /ch/ | chance |
| knock | /n/ to /sh/ | shock |

### ⇨ Lesson 33

| SAY: | CHANGE /*/ TO /*/ | THE WORD IS: |
|------|-------------------|--------------|
| sink | /s/ to /th/ | think |
| walk | /w/ to /ch/ | chalk |
| harp | /h/ to /sh/ | sharp |
| dunk | /d/ to /ch/ | chunk |
| love | /l/ to /sh/ | shove |
| born | /b/ to /th/ | thorn |

### ⇨ Lesson 34

| SAY: | CHANGE /*/ TO /*/ | THE WORD IS: |
|------|-------------------|--------------|
| clue | /k/ to /g/ | glue |
| brown | /b/ to /f/ | frown |
| frill | /f/ to /g/ | grill |
| brunch | /b/ to /k/ | crunch |
| slick | /s/ to /k/ | click |
| tweet | /t/ to /s/ | sweet |

✋ SUBSTITUTING HAND MOTION: Teacher holds 2 closed fists, touching at the thumbs, out in front to show the whole word. Right fist is the first sound, left fist is the rest of the word. Pull the right fist away when changing the first sound and lightly pound your fists together when you say the new word.

🍎

## TEACHER TIPS:

① If students struggle to change the intial sound, use felt or counters to represent the word:

⬛⬛ Pull the first rectangle away when changing the sound and replace it when saying the new word.

② /*/ Substitute the sound, not the letter name

# Substituting Initial Phonemes

LESSON FOCUS: When we substitute the initial phoneme, we change the first or initial sound to make a new word. In these lessons, I will say a word and we will substitute the first sound to make a new word.

Teacher Directions: I will say a word. You will repeat the word. We will substitute the first sound and you will tell me the new word.

Student Response: Students repeat the first word aloud, change the intial sound, and say the new word.

### ⇨ Lesson 35

| SAY: | CHANGE /*/ TO /*/ | THE WORD IS: |
|------|-------------------|--------------|
| pride | /p/ to /b/ | bride |
| slow | /s/ to /g/ | glow |
| brook | /b/ to /k/ | crook |
| twine | /t/ to /s/ | swine |
| clink | /k/ to /b/ | blink |
| front | /f/ to /g/ | grunt |

### ⇨ Lesson 36

| SAY: | CHANGE /*/ TO /*/ | THE WORD IS: |
|------|-------------------|--------------|
| grade | /g/ to /b/ | braid |
| clash | /k/ to /f/ | flash |
| fries | /f/ to /p/ | prize |
| groove | /g/ to /p/ | prove |
| twirl | /t/ to /s/ | swirl |
| blank | /b/ to /p/ | plank |

### ⇨ Lesson 37

| SAY: | CHANGE /*/ TO /*/ | THE WORD IS: |
|------|-------------------|--------------|
| blade | /b/ to /p/ | played |
| slide | /s/ to /g/ | glide |
| flip | /f/ to /s/ | slip |
| cried | /k/ to /f/ | fried |
| blot | /b/ to /s/ | slot |
| frail | /f/ to /b/ | brail |

### ⇨ Lesson 38

| SAY: | CHANGE /*/ TO /*/ | THE WORD IS: |
|------|-------------------|--------------|
| flock | /f/ to /k/ | clock |
| prey | /p/ to /g/ | gray |
| grace | /g/ to /b/ | brace |
| bright | /b/ to /f/ | fright |
| proud | /p/ to /k/ | crowd |
| plaid | /p/ to /g/ | glad |

🖐 SUBSTITUTING HAND MOTION: Teacher holds 2 closed fists, touching at the thumbs, out in front to show the whole word. Right fist is the first sound, left fist is the rest of the word. Pull the right fist away when changing the first sound and lightly pound your fists together when you say the new word.

### 🍎 TEACHER TIPS:

① If students struggle to change the intial sound, use felt or counters to represent the word:
   ■■ Pull the first rectangle away when changing the sound and replace it when saying the new word.

② /*/ Substitute the sound, not the letter name

# Substituting Initial Phonemes

We have worked on many lessons with substituting the first sound in a word to make a new word. Today, you will show me what you have learned.

Teacher Administration Directions: I will say a word. You will repeat the word. I will tell you the sound to substitute at the beginning, and you will tell me the new word.

Recording Directions: Record incorrect responses in the Student Response column. If correct, mark with a check or +

Student Name: _____     Date: _____

| | WORD: | CHANGE /*/ TO /*/ | CORRECT RESPONSE: | STUDENT RESPONSE |
|---|---|---|---|---|
| 1 | chair | /ch/ to /sh/ | share | |
| 2 | land | /l/ to /t/ | tanned | |
| 3 | yellow | /y/ to /f/ | fellow | |
| 4 | crane | /k/ to /b/ | brain | |
| 5 | flush | /f/ to /s/ | slush | |
| 6 | first | /f/ to /b/ | burst | |
| 7 | sink | /s/ to /th/ | think | |
| 8 | blow | /b/ to /g/ | glow | |
| 9 | plump | /p/ to /k/ | clump | |
| 10 | shower | /sh/ to /p/ | power | |
| | | | TOTAL SCORE: | /10 |

## SCORING GUIDE:

0-5 correct:  Review Substituting Intial Phonemes Lessons 29-38

6-8 correct: Review Substituting Intial Phonemes Lessons 34-38

9-10 correct:  Move on to Substituting Final Phonemes Lessons 39-48

# Anchor Lesson: Substituting Final Phonemes

**LESSON FOCUS:** The last sound we hear in a word is the final phoneme or sound. When we substitute the final sound, we can make a new word. In these lessons, I will say a word and we will substitute the final sound to make a new word.

## I DO:

I will show you how I can make a new word by changing or substituting the final sound in a word.

| made | T: Watch me. The word is make. I can segment make into 2 parts: /may - k/. The final sound is /k/. If I change /k/ to /d/, and the word is /may - d/, made. |
|------|--------|
| weed | T: Listen. Wheat. When I change /t/ to /d/, the word is /wee - d/, weed. |

## WE DO:

Let's try some words together. I will say the word. You will repeat the word. We will substitute the final sound and say the new word.

| nice | T: Say, night |
|------|--------|
|  | T & S: night |
|  | T: Change /t/ to /s/ and the word is? |
|  | T & S: nice |
| heart | T: Say, hard |
|  | T & S: hard |
|  | T: Change /d/ to /t/ and the word is? |
|  | T & S: heart |

## YOU DO:

I will say a word. You will repeat the word. I will tell you the sound to substitute at the end and you will tell me the new word.

| WORD: | CHANGE /*/ TO /*/ | THE WORD IS: |
|-------|--------|--------|
| side | /d/ to /t/ | sight |
| rice | /s/ to /z/ | rise |
| team | /m/ to /ch/ | teach |

**✋ SUBSTITUTING HAND MOTION:**

Teacher holds 2 closed fists, touching at the thumbs, out in front to show the whole word. Right fist is the first sound, left fist is the rest of the word. Pull the right fist away when changing the first sound and lightly pound your fists together when you say the new word.

# Substituting Final Phonemes

**LESSON FOCUS:** When we substitute the final phoneme, we change the last or final sound to make a new word. In these lessons, I will say a word and we will substitute the final sound to make a new word.

Teacher Directions: I will say a word. You will repeat the word. We will substitute the final sound to make a new word.

Student Response: Students repeat the first word aloud, change the final sound, and say the new word.

➩ **Lesson 39**

| SAY: | CHANGE /*/ TO /*/ | THE WORD IS: |
|------|-------------------|--------------|
| cook | /k/ to /d/ | could |
| pace | /s/ to /v/ | pave |
| herd | /d/ to /t/ | hurt |
| might | /t/ to /s/ | mice |
| lake | /k/ to /t/ | late |
| burn | /n/ to /d/ | bird |

➩ **Lesson 40**

| SAY: | CHANGE /*/ TO /*/ | THE WORD IS: |
|------|-------------------|--------------|
| corn | /n/ to /t/ | court |
| leave | /v/ to /s/ | lease |
| neat | /t/ to /d/ | need |
| crumb | /m/ to /sh/ | crush |
| coach | /ch/ to /n/ | cone |
| sleek | /k/ to /p/ | sleep |

➩ **Lesson 41**

| SAY: | CHANGE /*/ TO /*/ | THE WORD IS: |
|------|-------------------|--------------|
| graze | /z/ to /t/ | grate |
| swish | /sh/ to /ch/ | switch |
| brave | /v/ to /d/ | braid |
| grant | /t/ to /d/ | grand |
| brown | /n/ to /z/ | browse |
| start | /t/ to /v/ | starve |

➩ **Lesson 42**

| SAY: | CHANGE /*/ TO /*/ | THE WORD IS: |
|------|-------------------|--------------|
| stream | /m/ to /t/ | street |
| strike | /k/ to /v/ | strive |
| slight | /t/ to /d/ | slide |
| brake | /k/ to /n/ | brain |
| crowd | /d/ to /n/ | crown |
| snoop | /p/ to /z/ | snooze |

🖐 **SUBSTITUTING HAND MOTION:** Teacher holds 2 closed fists, touching at the thumbs, out in front to show the whole word. Right fist is the body of the word, left fist is the final sound. Pull the left fist away when changing the final sound and lightly pound your fists together when you say the new word.

🍎

**TEACHER TIPS:**

① If students struggle to change the final sound, use felt squares or counters to represent the word: ■ ■ Pull the last rectangle away when changing the sound and replace it when saying the new word.

② /*/ Say the sound, not the letter name

# Substituting Final Phonemes

**LESSON FOCUS:** When we substitute the final phoneme, we change the last or final sound to make a new word. In these lessons, I will say a word and we will substitute the final sound to make a new word.

Teacher Directions:  I will say a word.  You will repeat the word. We will substitute the final sound to make a new word.

Student Response:  Students repeat the first word aloud, change the final sound, and say the new word.

### ⇨ Lesson 43

| SAY: | CHANGE /*/ TO /*/ | THE WORD IS: |
|---|---|---|
| bark | /k/ to /n/ | barn |
| white | /t/ to /z/ | wise |
| whip | /p/ to /sh/ | wish |
| creek | /k/ to /m/ | cream |
| print | /t/ to /s/ | prince |
| reach | /ch/ to /th/ | wreath |

### ⇨ Lesson 44

| SAY: | CHANGE /*/ TO /*/ | THE WORD IS: |
|---|---|---|
| flag | /g/ to /sh/ | flash |
| curve | /v/ to /l/ | curl |
| chart | /t/ to /j/ | charge |
| grown | /n/ to /th/ | growth |
| pride | /d/ to /s/ | price |
| teeth | /th/ to /n/ | teen |

### ⇨ Lesson 45

| SAY: | CHANGE /*/ TO /*/ | THE WORD IS: |
|---|---|---|
| sweep | /p/ to /t/ | sweet |
| twine | /n/ to /s/ | twice |
| grade | /d/ to /n/ | grain |
| breathe | /th*/ to /z/ | breeze |
| pearl | /l/ to /s/ | purse |
| club | /b/ to /ch/ | clutch |

### ⇨ Lesson 46

| SAY: | CHANGE /*/ TO /*/ | THE WORD IS: |
|---|---|---|
| grant | /t/ to /d/ | grand |
| quick | /k/ to /z/ | quiz |
| swoop | /p/ to /n/ | swoon |
| heard | /d/ to /t/ | hurt |
| speed | /d/ to /ch/ | speech |
| swish | /sh/ to /m/ | swim |

✋ **SUBSTITUTING HAND MOTION:** Teacher holds 2 closed fists, touching at the thumbs, out in front to show the whole word.  Right fist is the body of the word, left fist is the final sound.  Pull the left fist away when changing the final sound and lightly pound your fists together when you say the new word.

🍎

### TEACHER TIPS:

① If students struggle to change the final sound, use felt squares or counters to represent the word:

■ ■  Pull the last rectangle away when changing the sound and replace it when saying the new word.

② /*/ Say the sound, not the letter name

# Substituting Final Phonemes

**LESSON FOCUS:** When we substitute the final phoneme, we change the last or final sound to make a new word. In these lessons, I will say a word and we will substitute the final sound to make a new word.

Teacher Directions: I will say a word. You will repeat the word. We will substitute the final sound to make a new word.

Student response: Students repeat the first word aloud, change the final sound, and say the new word.

## Lesson 47

| SAY: | CHANGE /*/ TO /*/ | THE WORD IS: |
|------|-------------------|--------------|
| scram | /m/ to /ch/ | scratch |
| welt | /t/ to /d/ | weld |
| mark | /k/ to /t/ | mart |
| snatch | /ch/ to /p/ | snap |
| bluff | /f/ to /sh/ | blush |
| proud | /d/ to /l/ | prowl |

## Lesson 48

| SAY: | CHANGE /*/ TO /*/ | THE WORD IS: |
|------|-------------------|--------------|
| swan | /n/ to /p/ | swap |
| height | /t/ to /v/ | hive |
| bend | /d/ to /ch/ | bench |
| scoop | /p/ to /l/ | school |
| stork | /k/ to /m/ | storm |
| bird | /d/ to /th/ | birth |

**SUBSTITUTING HAND MOTION:** Teacher holds 2 closed fists, touching at the thumbs, out in front to show the whole word. Right fist is the body of the word, left fist is the final sound. Pull the left fist away when changing the final sound and lightly pound your fists together when you say the new word.

## TEACHER TIPS:

1. If students struggle to change the final sound, use felt squares or counters to represent the word:

   ■ ■ Pull the last rectangle away when changing the sound and replace it when saying the new word.

2. /*/ Say the sound, not the letter name

# Substituting Final Phonemes

We have worked on many lessons with substituting the final sound in a word or to make a new word. Today, you will show me what you have learned.

Teacher Administration Directions: I will say a word. You will repeat the word. I will tell you the sound to substitute at the end, and you will tell me the new word.

Recording Directions: Record incorrect responses in the Student Response column. If correct, mark with a check or +

Student Name: _____          Date: _____

|   | WORD: | CHANGE /*/ TO /*/ | CORRECT RESPONSE: | STUDENT RESPONSE |
|---|-------|-------------------|-------------------|------------------|
| 1 | home | /m/ to /p/ | hope | |
| 2 | pork | /k/ to /ch/ | porch | |
| 3 | nurse | /s/ to /v/ | nerve | |
| 4 | sharp | /p/ to /k/ | shark | |
| 5 | board | /d/ to /n/ | born | |
| 6 | groom | /m/ to /p/ | group | |
| 7 | dive | /v/ to /s/ | dice | |
| 8 | wish | /sh/ to /p/ | whip | |
| 9 | carp | /p/ to /d/ | card | |
| 10 | coat | /t/ to /ch/ | coach | |
| | | | TOTAL SCORE: | /10 |

## SCORING GUIDE:

0-5 correct:  Review Substituting Final Phonemes Lessons 39-48

6-8 correct:  Review Substituting Final Phonemes Lessons 44-48

9-10 correct:  Move on to Substituting Medial Phonemes Lessons 49-58

# Anchor Lesson: Substituting Medial Phonemes

LESSON FOCUS: When we substitute the medial sound, we are changing the vowel sound we hear in a word to make a new word. The vowel sound may change from a short sound to a long sound, or change to an advanced vowel sound.

## I DO:

I will show you how I can make a new word by changing or substituting the medial (vowel) sound in a word.

| note | T: When I say the word not, the vowel or medial sound is /ŏ/. If I change /ŏ/ to /ō/, the word is n - ō - t, note. I changed the vowel from the short o sound to the long o sound. |
| --- | --- |
| ride | T: Listen. The word is read. When I change /ē/ to /ī/ the word is ride. r - ī - d, ride. |

## WE DO:

Let's try some words together. I will say the word. You will repeat the word. We will substitute the medial (vowel) sound and say the new word.

| said | T: Say, seed<br>T & S: seed<br>T: Change /ē/ to /ĕ/ and the word is?<br>T & S: said |
| --- | --- |
| get | T: Say, got<br>T & S: got<br>T: Change /ŏ/ to /ĕ/ and the word is?<br>T & S: get |

## YOU DO:

I will say a word. You will repeat the word. I will tell you the medial (vowel) sound to substitute and you will tell me the new word.

| WORD: | CHANGE /*/ TO /*/ | THE WORD IS: |
| --- | --- | --- |
| run | /ŭ/ to /ā/ | rain |
| weed | /ē/ to /ī/ | wide |
| pick | /ĭ/ to /ar/ | park |

### TEACHER TIP:

If students need additional support, use felt or counters to represent the medial/vowel sound: Pull the middle rectangle away when substituting the vowel sound and replace it to show the new sound and then say the word.

■ □ ■

# Substituting Medial Phonemes

LESSON FOCUS: When we substitute the medial sound, we are changing the vowel sound we hear in a word to make a new word.

Teacher Directions: I will say a word. You will repeat the word. We will substitute the medial or vowel sound to make a new word.

Student Response: Students repeat the first word aloud, change the vowel sound, and say the new word.

⊕ Lesson 49

| SAY: | CHANGE /*/ TO /*/ | THE WORD IS: |
|------|-------------------|--------------|
| brĕad | /ĕ/ to /ē/ | breed |
| plāne | /ā/ to /ă/ | plan |
| glŏb | /ŏ/ to /ō/ | globe |
| swēet | /ē/ to /ĕ/ | swĕat |
| cŭt | /ŭ/ to /ū/ | cute |
| mīle | /ī/ to /ĭ/ | mill |

⊕ Lesson 50

| SAY: | CHANGE /*/ TO /*/ | THE WORD IS: |
|------|-------------------|--------------|
| lăugh | /ă/ to /ī/ | life |
| cŭt | /ŭ/ to /ō/ | coat |
| frōze | /ō/ to /ē/ | freeze |
| crăsh | /ă/ to /ŭ/ | crush |
| brīde | /ī/ to /ĕ/ | bread |
| flŏck | /ŏ/ to /ā/ | flake |

### TEACHER TIP:

If students need additional support, use felt or counters to represent the medial/vowel sound: Pull the middle rectangle away when substituting the vowel sound and replace it to show the new sound and then say the word.

■ □ ■

# Substituting Medial Phonemes

LESSON FOCUS: When we substitute the medial sound, we are changing the vowel sound we hear in a word to make a new word.

Teacher Directions:  I will say a word.  You will repeat the word. We will substitute the medial or vowel sound to make a new word.

Student Response:  Students repeat the first word aloud, change the vowel sound, and say the new word.

## ⊙ Lesson 51

| SAY: | CHANGE /*/ TO /*/ | THE WORD IS: |
|---|---|---|
| slōpe | /ō/ to /ĭ/ | slip |
| rāte | /ā/ to /ī/ | right |
| crŭmb | /ŭ/ to /ē/ | cream |
| nĕt | /ĕ/ to /ō/ | note |
| mūte | /ū/ to /ĕ/ | met |
| thōse | /ō/ to /ē/ | these |

## ⊙ Lesson 52

| SAY: | CHANGE /*/ TO /*/ | THE WORD IS: |
|---|---|---|
| bŭn | /ŭ/ to /ar/ | barn |
| mīce | /ī/ to /oo/ | moose |
| spŏt | /ŏ/ to /ou/ | spout |
| toŭch | /ŭ/ to /or/ | torch |
| crowd | /ow/ to /or/ | cord |
| trāce | /ā/ to /oo/ | truce |

## ⊙ Lesson 53

| SAY: | CHANGE /*/ TO /*/ | THE WORD IS: |
|---|---|---|
| dark | /ar/ to /ĕ/ | deck |
| sāve | /ā/ to /er/ | serve |
| pēach | /ē/ to /or/ | porch |
| nĕt | /ĕ/ to /ō/ | note |
| start | /ar/ to /ā/ | state |
| gurgle | /ur/ to /ar/ | gargle |

## ⊙ Lesson 54

| SAY: | CHANGE /*/ TO /*/ | THE WORD IS: |
|---|---|---|
| took | /oo/ to /aw/ | talk |
| farm | /ar/ to /ir/ | firm |
| news | /ew/ to /oi/ | noise |
| mūle | /ū/ to /aw/ | mall |
| tĕn | /ĕ/ to /ow/ | town |
| point | /oi/ to /ā/ | paint |

### TEACHER TIP:

If students need additional support, use felt or counters to represent the medial/vowel sound: Pull the middle rectangle away when substituting the vowel sound and replace it to show the new sound and then say the word.

■ □ ■

# Substituting Medial Phonemes

**LESSON FOCUS:** When we substitute the medial sound, we are changing the vowel sound we hear in a word to make a new word.

Teacher Directions:  I will say a word.  You will repeat the word. We will substitute the medial or vowel sound to make a new word.

Student Response:  Students repeat the first word aloud, change the vowel sound, and say the new word.

### Lesson 55

| SAY: | CHANGE /*/ TO /*/ | THE WORD IS: |
|------|-------------------|--------------|
| band | /ă/ to /ĕ/ | bend |
| fern | /er/ to /ă/ | fan |
| rhyme | /ī/ to /oo/ | room |
| peach | /ē/ to /or/ | porch |
| math | /ă/ to /ou/ | mouth |
| work | /er/ to /aw/ | walk |

### Lesson 56

| SAY: | CHANGE /*/ TO /*/ | THE WORD IS: |
|------|-------------------|--------------|
| yarn | /ar/ to /aw/ | yawn |
| nice | /ī/ to /ur/ | nurse |
| seat | /ē/ to /or/ | sort |
| touch | /ŭ/ to /or/ | torch |
| join | /oi/ to /oo/ | June |
| shirt | /ir/ to /or/ | short |

### Lesson 57

| SAY: | CHANGE /*/ TO /*/ | THE WORD IS: |
|------|-------------------|--------------|
| goal | /ō/ to /ir/ | girl |
| dawn | /aw/ to /ow/ | down |
| turn | /ur/ to /or/ | torn |
| house | /ou/ to /or/ | horse |
| mine | /ī/ to /oo/ | moon |
| stork | /or/ to /ar/ | stark |

### Lesson 58

| SAY: | CHANGE /*/ TO /*/ | THE WORD IS: |
|------|-------------------|--------------|
| dorm | /or/ to /ĭ/ | dim |
| spoke | /ō/ to /oo/ | spook |
| wide | /ī/ to /er/ | word |
| truce | /oo/ to /ā/ | trace |
| just | /ŭ/ to /oi/ | joist |
| born | /or/ to /ar/ | barn |

### TEACHER TIP:

If students need additional support, use felt or counters to represent the medial/vowel sound: Pull the middle rectangle away when substituting the vowel sound and replace it to show the new sound and then say the word.

■ □ ■

# Substituting Medial Phonemes

We have worked on many lessons with substituting the medial (vowel) sound in a word to make a new word. Today, you will show me what you have learned.

Teacher Administration Directions: I will say a word. You will repeat the word. I will tell you the medial (vowel) sound to substitute, and you will tell me the new word.

Recording Directions: Record incorrect responses in the Student Response column. If correct, mark with a check or +

Student Name: _____     Date: _____

|   | WORD: | CHANGE /*/ TO /*/ | CORRECT RESPONSE: | STUDENT RESPONSE |
|---|-------|-------------------|-------------------|------------------|
| 1 | mouse | /ou/ to /oo/ | moose | |
| 2 | point | /oi/ to /ā/ | paint | |
| 3 | supper | /ŭ/ to /oo/ | super | |
| 4 | minor | /ī/ to /ă/ | manner | |
| 5 | many | /ĕ/ to /ŭ/ | money | |
| 6 | turtle | /ur/ to /ī/ | title | |
| 7 | pouring | /or/ to /er/ | purring | |
| 8 | beat | /ē/ to /ō/ | boat | |
| 9 | trip | /ĭ/ to /ă/ | trap | |
| 10 | coin | /oi/ to /ō/ | cone | |
| | | | TOTAL SCORE: | /10 |

SCORING GUIDE:

0-5 correct: Review Substituting Medial Phonemes Lessons 49-58

6-8 correct: Review Substituting Medial Phonemes Lessons 54-58

9-10 correct: Move on to Substituting Various Phonemes Lessons 59-70

# Anchor Lesson: Substituting Various Sounds

LESSON FOCUS: We have practiced changing sounds in the beginning, middle and end of words. In the next lessons, we will be substitute or change a sound in a word. You will need to listen carefully to identify the location of the sound in the word before we change it to the new sound.

## I DO:

I will show you how I can make a new word by changing or substituting any sound a word.

| odor | Watch me. The word is over. When I change /v/ to /d/, the new word is /ō/ - /der/, odor. |
| slept | Watch me. The word is slipped. When I change /ĭ/ to /ĕ/, the new word is slept. |

## WE DO:

Let's try some words together. I will say the word. You will repeat the word. We will substitute a sound and say the new word. Remember to listen carefully for where the sound is in the word.

| corn | T: Say, cone |
| | T & S: cone |
| | T: Change /ō/ to /or/ and the word is? |
| | T & S: corn |
| shirt | T: Say, brand |
| | T & S: brand |
| | T: Change /d/ to /ch/ and the word is? |
| | T & S: branch |

## YOU DO:

I will say word. You will repeat the word. I will tell you what sound to substitute and you will tell me the new word.

| WORD: | CHANGE /*/ TO /*/ | THE WORD IS: |
|---|---|---|
| glue | /l/ to /r/ | grew |
| swell | /w/ to /p/ | spell |
| actor | /k/ to /f/ | after |

🍎

### TEACHER TIP:

If students need additional support, use felt, elkonin boxes or counters to represent the the location of the sound: Pull the visual away that represents the sound be substituted and replace it to show the new sound and then say the word.

# Substituting Various Phonemes

LESSON FOCUS: We will substitute a sound in different places throughout a word.  You will have to listen carefully to identify the location of the sound in the word before we change it to a new sound.

Teacher Directions:   I will say a word.  You will repeat the word. We will substitute a sound to make a new word.

Student Response:  Students repeat the first word aloud, change a sound, and say the new word.

## ⇨ Lesson 59

| SAY: | CHANGE /*/ TO /*/ | THE WORD IS: |
|---|---|---|
| clam | /l/ to /r/ | cram |
| grateful | /t/ to /s/ | graceful |
| smash | /m/ to /l/ | slash |
| taking | /k/ to /m/ | taming |
| nature | /ā/ to /ur/ | nurture |
| frame | /r/ to /l/ | flame |

## ⇨ Lesson 60

| SAY: | CHANGE /*/ TO /*/ | THE WORD IS: |
|---|---|---|
| oval | /v/ to /p/ | opal |
| lady | /d/ to /s/ | lacy |
| clown | /l/ to /r/ | crown |
| cat | /ă/ to /aw/ | caught |
| candle | /d/ to /s/ | cancel |
| had | /ă/ to /ar/ | hard |

## ⇨ Lesson 61

| SAY: | CHANGE /*/ TO /*/ | THE WORD IS: |
|---|---|---|
| bench | /ch/ to /t/ | bent |
| buddy | /d/ to /n/ | bunny |
| sleeve | /v/ to /p/ | sleep |
| slick | /l/ to /t/ | stick |
| servant | /v/ to /p/ | serpent |
| slipper | /p/ to /k/ | slicker |

## ⇨ Lesson 62

| SAY: | CHANGE /*/ TO /*/ | THE WORD IS: |
|---|---|---|
| send | /ĕ/ to /ă/ | sand |
| pushing | /sh/ to /d/ | pudding |
| bent | /b/ to /l/ | lent |
| sway | /w/ to /t/ | stay |
| pedal | /d/ to /b/ | pebble |
| wish | /sh/ to /th/ | with |

### TEACHER TIP:

If students need additional support, use felt, elkonin boxes or counters to represent the the location of the sound: Pull the visual away that represents the sound be substituted and replace it to show the new sound and then say the word.

# Substituting Various Phonemes

LESSON FOCUS: We will substitute a sound in different places throughout a word. You will have to listen carefully to identify the location of the sound in the word before we change it to a new sound.

Teacher Directions:   I will say a word.  You will repeat the word. We will substitute a sound to make a new word.

Student Response:  Students repeat the first word aloud, change a sound, and say the new word.

⇨ Lesson 63

| SAY: | CHANGE /*/ TO /*/ | THE WORD IS: |
|------|-------------------|--------------|
| loft | /f/ to /s/ | lost |
| swing | /w/ to /l/ | sling |
| glaze | /l/ to /r/ | graze |
| angle | /g/ to /k/ | ankle |
| switch | /ch/ to /sh/ | swish |
| funny | /n/ to /z/ | fuzzy |

⇨ Lesson 64

| SAY: | CHANGE /*/ TO /*/ | THE WORD IS: |
|------|-------------------|--------------|
| tiger | /g/ to /t/ | tighter |
| west | /s/ to /n/ | went |
| scan | /k/ to /p/ | span |
| ripple | /p/ to /d/ | riddle |
| tend | /d/ to /t/ | tent |
| flight | /l/ to /r/ | fright |

⇨ Lesson 65

| SAY: | CHANGE /*/ TO /*/ | THE WORD IS: |
|------|-------------------|--------------|
| manner | /n/ to /t/ | matter |
| broom | /r/ to /l/ | bloom |
| crab | /b/ to /sh/ | crash |
| hockey | /k/ to /l/ | holly |
| math | /ă/ to /ou/ | mouth |
| barn | /n/ to /k/ | bark |

⇨ Lesson 66

| SAY: | CHANGE /*/ TO /*/ | THE WORD IS: |
|------|-------------------|--------------|
| later | /t/ to /z/ | lazer |
| moose | /oo/ to /ou/ | mouse |
| snore | /n/ to /k/ | score |
| better | /ĕ/ to /ŭ/ | butter |
| torch | /or/ to /ē/ | teach |
| puddle | /ŭ/ to /ă/ | paddle |

🍎

## TEACHER TIP:

If students need additional support, use felt, elkonin boxes or counters to represent the the location of the sound: Pull the visual away that represents the sound be substituted and replace it to show the new sound and then say the word.

# Substituting Various Phonemes

LESSON FOCUS: We will substitute a sound in different places throughout a word. You will have to listen carefully to identify the location of the sound in the word before we change it to a new sound.

Teacher Directions:   I will say a word.  You will repeat the word. We will substitute a sound to make a new word.

Student Response:  Students repeat the first word aloud, change a sound, and say the new word.

## Lesson 67

| SAY: | CHANGE /*/ TO /*/ | THE WORD IS: |
|------|-------------------|--------------|
| glum | /m/ to /v/ | glove |
| climb | /k/ to /s/ | slime |
| center | /t/ to /d/ | sender |
| shut | /ŭ/ to /or/ | short |
| tart | /ar/ to /au/ | taught |
| wishing | /sh/ to /n/ | winning |

## Lesson 68

| SAY: | CHANGE /*/ TO /*/ | THE WORD IS: |
|------|-------------------|--------------|
| wind | /d/ to /s/ | wince |
| staple | /p/ to /b/ | stable |
| snake | /k/ to /l/ | snail |
| slim | /l/ to /w/ | swim |
| rising | /z/ to /t/ | writing |
| starry | /ar/ to /or/ | story |

## Lesson 69

| SAY: | CHANGE /*/ TO /*/ | THE WORD IS: |
|------|-------------------|--------------|
| bird | /ir/ to /or/ | board |
| cheaper | /p/ to /t/ | cheater |
| quote | /ō/ to /ī/ | quite |
| sleep | /l/ to /w/ | sweep |
| praise | /p/ to /g/ | graze |
| truth | /th/ to /p/ | troop |

## Lesson 70

| SAY: | CHANGE /*/ TO /*/ | THE WORD IS: |
|------|-------------------|--------------|
| eager | /g/ to /t/ | eater |
| fruit | /r/ to /l/ | flute |
| sling | /l/ to /t/ | sting |
| prĕsent | /r/ to /l/ | pleasant |
| protect | /t/ to /j/ | prōject |
| splint | /l/ to /r/ | sprint |

# What Comes Next?

Explicit phonemic awareness instruction is just one piece of a literacy intervention. It is essential for learners to reach phoneme proficiency, however, there is much work to be done alongside and beyond building that foundation.

After completing the lessons within the Bridge the Gap Intervention Curriculum, teachers may do one or all of the following:

**RE-ASSESS:**

Re-administer the placement assessment on pages 5-12. Record student scores in the indicated post column to evaluate student progress and inform further instruction. If additional assessments are needed, strand assessments for phoneme manipulation can be found on our website at www.heggerty.org/downloads.

**RE-TEACH:**

Use the post- assessment to identify specific skills that may require additional time. If students are not yet proficient, consider providing additional scaffolding by creating more "We Do" opportunities within the lessons.

As students progress toward proficiency, remove scaffolded support, such as visuals and hand motions.

**CONNECT:**

Phonemic awareness is just one piece of literacy instruction and intervention. It is essential that students see the connection between the oral and auditory work of phonemic awareness and print (phonics). Create opportunities for the connection of PA, word study and application to connected text (decodable or controlled).

**PHONEMIC PROFICIENCY:**

After receiving explicit instruction in phonemic awareness, you may find your students have reached phonemic proficiency but still struggle with decoding and encoding.

Phonemic awareness instruction may be removed from their intervention, however, they will still need explicit phonics instruction with the opportunity to apply those skills to connected text.

According to the National Reading Panel Report (2000), "Teachers should recognize that acquiring phonemic awareness is a means rather than an end. PA is not acquired for its own sake but rather for its value in helping learners understand and use the alphabetic system to read and write."

"However, it is also clear that this instruction is only one small part of an effective overall reading curriculum. Good training in phonological awareness should be combined with systematic, direct, and explicit instruction in phonics, as well as rich experiences with language and literature..." (Torgesen & Mathes, 2000)